D1343839

THE WIT & WISDOM OF
CRICKET

Published in 2012 by Prion
an imprint of the Carlton Publishing Group
20 Mortimer Street
London W1T 3JW

ISBN: 978-1-85375-862-1

Printed in China

THE WIT & WISDOM OF
CRICKET

**More than 800 amusing, enlightening and
downright unsportsmanlike quotations**

PRION

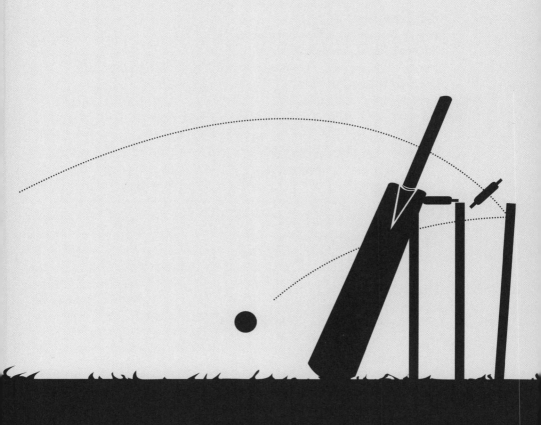

Contents

There are over 1,000 quotes in this collection. Each quote that appears is numbered (i.e.•123).
These numbers run sequentially throughout the book. Use the index at the back to find players of,
or commentators on, the game of Cricket. The index is listed in alphabetical order by surname.

To Dad. Sorry about the fence.
And to Wellsy,
a cricketer and a gent.

Cricket excites enormous passion and zeal in those who follow it. Many have tried — and mostly failed — to simplify its complexities and get to the very essence of the game.

What is human life but a game of cricket?

The Duke of Dorset, 1777 •26

If ye Wicket is Bowled down, it's Out.

First code of rules, 1744. Laws for Ye Strikers •1

11

Cricket is first and foremost a dramatic spectacle.
It belongs with theatre, ballet, opera and dance.

C.L.R. James •2

The cricket world, surely, is as crazy
and inconsistent as the outside one.

Jack Fingleton •3

Cricket is battle and service and sport and art. *Douglas Jardine* •4

Cricket is a liberal education in itself, and demands temper,
justice and perseverance. There is more teaching in the playground
than in the schoolrooms and a lesson better worth learning often.
For there can be no good or enjoyable cricket without enthusiasm
— without sentiment, one may almost say; a quality that enriches
life and refines it; gives it... zest. *Andrew Lang, in K.S. Ranjitsinhji's*
The Book of Cricket, *1897* •5

Cricket is a subtle game. In form and appearance it
can be gentle, even idyllic, yet violence is always there.

Mihir Bose •6

**Cricket is a game which the British, not being a spiritual people,
had to invent in order to have some concept of eternity.**
Lord Mancroft, Bees in Some Bonnets, 1979 •7

Cricket is certainly among the most powerful
links which keep our Empire together. It is one
of the greatest contributions which the British
people have made to the cause of humanity.
K.S. Ranjitsinhji •8

Cricket, however, has more in it than mere
efficiency. There is something called the
spirit of cricket, which cannot be defined.

Lionel, Lord Tennyson, Sticky Wickets, 1950 •9

There can be raw pain and bleeding where so many thousands
see the inevitable ups and downs of only a game.

C.L.R. James, **Beyond a Boundary, 1963** •10

The game preys on doubt. It is a precarious game. Form, luck,
confidence are transitory things. It's never easy to
work out why they have so inexplicably deserted you.

Peter Roebuck, **It Never Rains, 1984** •11

To go to a cricket match for nothing but cricket is as though a man were to go into an inn for nothing but drink. *Neville Cardus,* Autobiography, 1947 •12

This strange urge to wear long white trousers and
a multi-coloured cap — well, its not natural is it?

Marcus Berkman in **Rain Men, 1995** •13

It is a brave pastime, a game for soldiers,
for each tries to strike the other with the
ball, and it is but a small stick with
which you ward it off. *Arthur Conan Doyle* •14

A game is exactly what is made of it
by the character of the men playing it.

Sir Neville Cardus, **Good Days** *(1934)* •15

The key to the health and prosperity of the game
is embedded not in rules and regulations but in
the hearts and minds of the cricketers of today.

E.W. Swanton, **A History of Cricket, Volume Two (1962),** •16

We... do agree to meet upon Heworth Moor
every Tuesday and Friday morning at 4 o'clock
until the Fifth day of September next, for
the purpose of playing cricket.

York C.C's inaugural rules, 1784 •25

First-class cricket is a subtle as well as a strenuous
game. It is a thing of leisure, albeit of leisure today
not easily found or arranged; a three-act play not
a slapstick turn. *R.C. Robertson-Glasgow* •18

You will do well to love it, it is more free from anything sordid, anything dishonourable, than any game in the world. To play it keenly, honourably, generously, self-sacrificing is a moral lesson in itself, and the class-room is full of God's own air and children. Foster it, my brothers, so that it may attract all who can find the time to play it; protect it from anything that would sully it, so that it may grow in favour with all men.

Lord Harris's speech reported in The Times, *1931* •19

The bowler has ten aides in the field, but they are helpless to act until that swift cut and thrust, that intensely private moment between batsman and bowler, is done. This numerical advantage of players to the bowling side, however, creates a situation which is almost unique to cricket. It makes batting, consequently the scoring of runs, an act of defiance by one man against a vastly superior force who control the ball at all times, except in that split second when it touches the bat.

Geoffrey Moorhouse, The Best-Loved Game, *1979* •20

What do they know of cricket
who only cricket know? *C.L.R. James* •21

It (cricket) is a most notorious and shameless breach of the
laws, as it gives the most open encouragement to gambling.
The British Champion, 1743 •22

Cricket is certainly a very
good and wholesome exercise,
yet it may be abused if either
great or little people make
it their business.

Gentlemen's magazine, 1743 •23

To many writers the period leading up to the Great War in 1914 were the halcyon days of cricket. They were the days of amateur and professional toe to toe on flawless wickets in idyllic surroundings during perfect summers. Or not. But it's nice to pretend…

How those brawn-faced fellows of farmers would drink to our success! And then what stuff they had to drink! Punch! Not your new Ponche a la Romaine or Ponche a la Groseille, or your modern cat-lap milk punch — punch — punch be devilled. But good, unsophisticated John Bull stuff — stark! — that would stand on end — punch that would make a cat speak!
John Nyren, recalling cricket at Hambledon in the 1780s •27

19

A wet day, only three members present, nine bottles of wine.

Extract from early minutes of Hambledon Club •28

They were backbone players, ready to go till they dropped and never sick or sorry in a match.

John Bowyer (Surrey, The Players, England) on the Hambledon XI •29

Last week, at Sileby feast, the women so far forgot themselves as to enter a game of cricket, and by their deportment as well as frequent applications to the tankard, they rendered themselves objects such as no husband, parent or lover could contemplate with any degree of satisfaction.

Nottingham Review, 1833 •30

It was a study for Phidias to see Beldham rise to strike; the grandeur of the attitude, the settled composure of the look, the piercing lightening of the eye, the rapid glance of the bat, were electrical. Men's hearts throbbed within them, their cheeks turned pale and red. Michael Angelo (sic) should have painted him.

Rev John Mitford, **The Gentleman's Magazine, 1833** •31

Cricket grounds be laid out at
each end of the barrack stations
throughout the United Kingdom
for the use of officers and privates.

Order by the Duke of Wellington, Commander in Chief, 1841 •32

It's more than a game.
It's an institution.

Thomas Hughes, **Tom Brown's Schooldays, 1857** •33

On the cricket grounds of the Empire is fostered
the spirit of never knowing when you are beaten,
of playing for your side and not for yourself, and
of never giving up a game as lost… the future of
cricket and the Empire is so inseparably connected.

Lord Hawke, in introduction to **Warner's Imperial Cricket** •34

Coaching which is good, simply sharpens up
a player, as wide travel and experience will.
A.E. Knight, **The Complete Cricketer, 1906** •35

The cricket player is not an actor on a stage, merely
a personality to be lost in the creation of a poet's brain
or a playwright's mind; he is himself the poet and the
playwright. *A.E. Knight,* **The Complete Cricketer 1906** •36

Captaincy by committee on or off the field is lamentable.

A.E. Knight, **The Complete Cricketer, 1906** •37

The Battle of Britain was now in full swing, but we
decided to carry on with the game as a number of
boys had put their names down and I didn't want
to disappoint them. *Henry Grierson, founder and Honorary
Secretary of The Forty Club, on their match v Public Schools at
Richmond, August 1940* •38

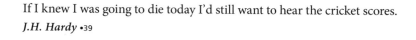

If I knew I was going to die today I'd still want to hear the cricket scores.
J.H. Hardy •39

It was so late in the season that some of the best amateurs were spending their holidays far away from cricket grounds and would be, of course, out of practice. *Lord Harris on the difficulties of recruiting the England side to play Australia at The Oval, 1880, the first England v Australia Test* •40

This modern scoffing at tradition is a product of super-democracy. Tradition is a good thing. It's what takes a regiment through hell.

Pelham Warner •41

Cricket is a stalwart Goliath striding across the British Empire. MCC is his devoted wife, anxious only to further his best interest. Cricket and MCC will never be divorced. Therefore, they are a very old-fashioned couple but will go on happily united as long as the game is played.

Sir Home Gordon, to Cross Arrows dinner, Lord's, 1929 •42

23

Pray God no professional may ever captain England. *Lord Hawke* •43

It is one of the ironies of our first-class game that the seventh Lord Hawke, who in his way tried hard to give the professionals of his day an improved status, was held up to such scorn. One stray, ill-chosen sentence of his, in which he rhetorically prayed to God that no professional would ever captain England, looked haughty and insensitive in print, and summoned up bitter emotions from the less privileged.

David Foot, Cricket's Unholy Trinity, 1985 •44

I have heard some English captains speak to their professionals like dogs.

Joe Darling, Australian captain, 1902 •45

In all this Australian team, there are barely one or two who would be accepted as public school men. *C.B. Fry on the 1938 Australians* •46

No games have given me more pleasure than these tussles with the professors.

G.L. Jessop on the Gentleman v Players matches •47

Look, Nastase, we used to have a famous cricket match in the country called Gentlemen Versus Players. The Gentlemen were put down on the scorecard as 'Mister' because they were gentlemen. By no stretch of the imagination can anybody call you a gentleman.

Trader Horn, Wimbledon umpire, on being asked to address Ilie Nastase as 'Mr Nastase' •48

25

Few things are more deeply rooted in the collective imagination of the English than the village cricket match. It stirs a romantic illusion about the rustic way of life, it suggests a tranquil and unchanging order in an age of bewildering flux, and it persuades a lot of townsfolk that that is where they would rather be.
Geoffrey Moorhouse, **The Best-Loved Game, 1979** •49

Villagers do not think village cricket is funny.

John Arlott, foreword to Gerald Howat's **Village Cricket, 1981** •50

The single most important change has been the decline of the personality player and the rise of the professional attitude... it is a product of the times, a tangent from Trade Unionism. *Colin Cowdrey, 1976* •52

This is a Test match. It's not Old Reptonians versus Lymeswold, one off the mark and jolly good show.

David Gower, refuses to condemn West Indies' short-pitched bowling in 1984 •53

The driest and most rigid-limbed chap I ever knew, his skin was like the rind of an old oak, and as sapless. I have seen his knuckles handsomely knocked about from Harris's bowling; but never saw any blood on his hands — you might just as well attempt to phlebotomize a mummy. *John Nyren,* **The Cricketers of My Time,** *on Tom Walker* **(Hambledon, 1780s)** •54

After leaving Harrow... he went up to Oxford with the sole intention of 'playing cricket' (as he said), but, on being informed that he would have to undertake certain lessons, and having no liking for books, he made rather a hurried departure. *W.E. Howard on 'Monkey' Hornby of Lancashire and England in the 1880s* •56

Perhaps Harris was a bit of a dictator, but he was eminently just and fair.

Sir Pelham Warner on Lord Harris, **Long Innings, 1951** •57

...conducted his entire career as though he were conducting a cavalry charge against the forces of darkness, when in fact he never did much more than tilt against windmills.

Benny Green on A.C. MacLaren, **The Lord's Companion, 1987** •58

A tall, rather slim figure, but lissom, wiry, and full of vitality; a very high action and an atmosphere of undisguised hostility, and a subtle and unresting brain behind it all.

H.S. Altham, **A History of Cricket, 1928,** *on F.R. Spofforth (Australia)* •59

In all games where there is any pecuniary benefit to be derived, the professional invariably beats the amateur, and the reason is easily found in that the professional works much harder than the amateur. *FR Spofforth.* •60

There is a love — and usually a sadness — at the heart of a cult. Victor Trumper was the first tragic hero of Australian cricket.

David Frith, Archie Jackson, 1987 •64

He [Tom Emmett] was the smile on the face of cricket, a smile that has hardly faded even now in these days of less mirthful men in more immaculate flannels.

Peter Thomas, Yorkshire Cricketers 1839 –1939, *1973* •65

29

Robinson seemed to be made out of the stuff of Yorkshire county. I imagine that the Lord one day gathered together a heap of Yorkshire clay and breathed into it and said 'Emmott Robinson, go and bowl at the pavilion end for Yorkshire.' *Neville Cardus* •66

He was one of the last of his kind — and certainly the finest specimen of it — the amateurs, the smiling gentlemen of games, intensely devoted to the skill and the struggle but always with a certain gaiety, romantic at heart but classical in style.

J.B. Priestley on C.B. Fry, **The English, 1973** •67

If you like a white sun hat always carry one with you. C.B. Fry played some of his greatest innings in a sun hat.

Jack Bond, Lancashire CCC manager, 1985 •68

Victor Trumper had the greatest charm and two strokes for every ball.

C.B. Fry •69

When you're a batter and a bowler, you enjoy yourself twice as much.

George Hirst. •69

What can you have better than a nice green field, with the wickets set up, and to go out and do the best for your side?

George Hirst •70

In George Hirst's cricket we have, almost perfectly displayed, the outlook of the true cavalier: gay and always attacking.

A.A. Thomson, Hirst and Rhodes, 1959 •71

We don't play this game for fun.

Wilfred Rhodes •72

It was my grandfather who first told me about him. He once walked the 30 miles to Bradford to see Rhodes play and he never forgot it.

Michael Parkinson, Cricket Mad, 1969 •73

If a batsman thinks it's spinning, then it's spinning. *Wilfred Rhodes* •74

Barnes scythed through batsmen because he believed in the divine right of Barnes.

Bernard Hollowood, Cricket on the Brain, 1970 •75

33

It is very important for a man who wishes to have a good season to take regular exercise. *K.S. Ranjitsinhji* •76

After being warned for years as to the danger of playing back on a fast wicket, and especially to fast bowling, it came as rather a surprise to see the great Indian batsman transgressing against a principle so firmly fixed in one's mind.

G.L. Jessop, on Ranji •77

Find out where the ball is. Go there. Hit it.

Ranji's three precepts of batsmanship •78

There was nothing
ferocious or brutal
in Spooner's batting,
it was all courtesy
and breeding.
Neville Cardus on R.H. Spooner •79

He never
seemed to
make runs
– they came.
G.L. Jessop on Arthur Shrewsbury •61

For Constantine made himself for all predictable time into
the great representative symbol of West Indian cricket,
partly by the accident of history and partly by the sheer
stunning impact of skill and personality.

Ronald Mason, **Sing All A Green Willow, 1967** •80

35

Ranji travelled in the sixth coach and Fry and
Jackson in the seventh (but W G Grace, although
captain of Sheffield's XI, was not thus honoured,
his lack of public school and university background
seemingly making him less socially acceptable
than than the three young Varsity Blues).

Anthony Meredith, The Demon and the Lobster, 1987 •81

He revolutionised cricket. He turned it from an accomplishment into a science.

K.S. Ranjitsinhji, The Jubilee Book of Cricket, 1897 *on W.G. Grace* •82

Admission 3d; If Dr. W.G. Grace plays, Admission 6d.

Notice outside grounds in 1870s •84

I should like to say that good batsmen are born, not made; but my long experience comes up before me, and tells me that it is not so. *W.G. Grace,* Cricket, 1981 •85

The first ball I sent whizzing through his whiskers; after that he kept hitting me off his blinkin' ear 'ole for four.

Ernest Jones, playing against W.G., 1896 •86

The Majority of our side were thoroughly in accord with the (umpire's) decision, but nothing would shake 'WG's' contention, and for the rest of the day we all went about our tasks in hushed silence.

G.L. Jessop on Grace's response to having a run-out appeal turned down after A.C. MacLaren trod on his wicket, Lancashire v Gloucestershire, Old Trafford, 1896 •87

I thought if I didn't go in tonight I'd never get in at all against that bowling.

Grace's explanation for not sending in a night-watchman in difficult conditions •88

After all I've done for you, that's what you do to me!

W.G. Grace, to Palmer, the Kent wicket-keeper, who stumped him minutes after the Doctor had given him stitches for a head wound caused by a bouncer •89

In order to slim, he drank cider, although latter-day dieticians might look askance at a GP supping scrumpy to reduce his waistline.

Eric Midwinter, W.G. Grace, 1981 •90

What, are you going, Doctor? There's still one stump standing.

Charles Kortright, Essex pace bowler, to W.G. Grace after bowling him •91

The champion had been asked to name the greatest batsman with whom he had been associated in the 50 years of his unique cricketing life. With a stroke of his silvery beard and an inimitable twinkle of those bright eyes from behind their bushy brows, he had, with a little persuasion, agreed that he himself should be hors concours, but as regard the proxime accessit, his answer came quick and decided: Give me Arthur!

W.G. accords Arthur Shrewsbury the accolade of second best to himself, H.S. Altham, A History of Cricket, Volume One, 1926 •92

Uncle Ted's proximity to the batsman, apart from the chances of a catch, was no inconceivable asset to the bowler. He kept up a running commentary with the batsman, which, in the case of some, was apt to prevent that entire concentration of thought which is so requisite for success.

G.L. Jessop, in The Cricketer. *Uncle Ted was Grace the elder's nickname* •93

It may not be cricket, but it's four.

E.M. Grace pulling a ball from outside off-stump, which was considered unethical in the mid-nineteenth century •94

Grace, then, is the Beethoven of cricket, bridging the old game and the modern just as Beethoven bridged the classical and the romantic in music.

Gerry Cotter, The Ashes Captains, 1989 •95

Test Cricket Test matches are the true arbiter of a player's worth. Fears that one-day cricket would take over have been allayed by some ferociously contested Test series in recent years. One-day cricket has had its great moments — but none to live in the memory the epic struggles of the great Test matches.

In affectionate Remembrance
of ENGLISH CRICKET which
died at the Oval on 29th August, 1882.
Deeply lamented by a large circle
of
sorrowing Friends and Acquaintances R.I.P.
N.B. – The body will be cremated, and
the Ashes taken to Australia.

Sporting Times *obituary which began the story of 'The Ashes'* •96

41

If you ever come to England and your bowlers
are as good there as they are here, you will make
a name for yourselves. *W.G. Grace, on tour of Australia, 1873* •97

They are capital winners out here, but I'm afraid that
I cannot apply the same adjective to them as losers.
Lord Harris on Australians •98

Well, we shall win the Ashes — but we may lose a Dominion.

Rockley Wilson on Jardine's appointment as MCC Captain in Australia, 1932/3 •99

He can be a powerful friend but a ruthless enemy.
He gives no quarter and asks none. He is a fighter,
every inch of him. He will see a job through, no matter
what the consequences, and will never admit defeat.
Bill Bowes, Express Deliveries, *1949. On D.R. Jardine* •100

I don't want to see you Mr Warner. There are two teams out there; one is trying to play cricket and the other is not.

Bill Woodfull to Pelham Warner, the England manager, Adelaide, 1932-33 •101

Bodyline bowling has assumed such proportions
as to menace the best interests of the game, making
protection of the body by the batsmen the main consideration.
This is causing intensely bitter feeling between the players
as well as injury. In our opinion it is unsportsmanlike. Unless
stopped at once it is likely to upset the friendly
relationships existing between Australia and England.
*Text of cable from Australian Cricket Board to MCC,
following Adelaide Test, 1933* •102

So used are the batsman to being on top that when a form of attack is evolved to put bowlers on terms again up rises a wall of protest.

Bruce Harris, Jardine Justified *1933* •103

His Excellency is a conscientious objector.

*Douglas Jardine's sanguine view of the Nawab of Pataudi refusal to join the leg-side field,
1932/3* •104

If I happen to get hit out there Dad,
keep Mum from jumping the fence
and laying into those pommy bowlers.

Stan McCabe, resuming his innings of 187 in the Bodyline series,
1932/3 •105

I've never felt so glad in my life as when I saw who was coming in.
Peter May on Cyril Washbrook's entrance in his comeback match, after a five-
year absence with England 17-3 against Australia at Headingley, 1956 •110

When the ambition of a lifetime is fulfilled,
when a schoolboy's dream comes true,
something has gone from one's life.

Neville Cardus on covering an Ashes series abroad
for the first time in 1936-37, aged 49 •107

Leg-theory, even as bowled by Larwood, came as a natural
evolution in the game. There was nothing sinister about it
and nothing sinister was intended. *Bill Bowes, 1949* •108

If I played and missed he was standing at the other end, grinning. If I tried a really big heave and made no contact he would just lean on his bat and laugh out loud.

Graham Dilley's memories of the same match •114

> Only a drama that is allowed to unfold over five days could permit such a twist in the plot so wild as to be almost unthinkable.
>
> *Paul Fitzpatrick (Leeds, 1981) on the extraordinary Headingley test of that year* •115

Test cricket is not a light-hearted business, especially that between England and Australia.

Sir Donald Bradman, Farewell to Cricket *(1950)* •116

> There are few remaining English prophets in Australia forecasting anything but doom, but for heavens sake let's not panic. England have only three major problems. They can't bat, they can't bowl and they can't field.
>
> *Martin Johnson,* The Independent, *shortly before England won the Ashes in 1986-87* •117

Hobbs, Hammond and Broad: it doesn't quite ring true, does it?

Chris Broad matches some august names by scoring a hundred in three successive Ashes Tests •118

I admire the Australians' approach to the game; they have the utmost ability for producing that little extra, or instilling into the opposition an inferiority complex that can have, and has had, a crushing effect. Australians have no inhibitions. *Sir Leonard Hutton,* **Just My Story,** *1956* •111

The traditional dress of the Australian cricketer is the baggy green cap on the head and the chip on the shoulder.

Simon Barnes •121

With the possible exception of Rolf Harris, no other Australian has inflicted more pain and grief on Englishmen since Don Bradman.

Mike Walters of the **Daily Mirror** *on Steve Waugh's retirement* •122

We find it both amusing and amazing how they always talk it up with about 12 months to go, telling everyone that they've finally got the team to beat us. *Oh, Glen* •123

They have plenty of ability with no grunt, or they have plenty of grunt with no ability.

Merv Hughes on England cricketers, 2005. Presumably he stopped watching England in about 2001. •124

England will lose the five-Test series 3-0 and the margin will be worse for them if it doesn't rain. If you put the players from Australia and England up against each other it is embarrassing. There is no contest between them on an individual or team basis. *Jeff Thomson. Whatever.* •125

He's like a net bowler when you compare him to McGrath and Kasprowicz.

Jeff Thomson on Matthew Hoggard, pre Ashes 2005 •126

This England team, while they are better and on track, I can't see them beating this Australian team in a game.

A less offensive, but still incorrect assessment, from Ian Healy •127

When appealing, the Australians
make a statement; we ask a question.

Vic Marks •112

I think I was saying 3-0 or 4-0 about
twelve months ago, thinking there
might be a bit of rain around. But
with the weather as it is at the
moment, I have to say 5-0.

Oh, Glen, oh dear •129

If Australia get away to a good start then England have got
no chance. They have got to be competitive in that first test at
Lord's or else it's goodnight.

Terry Alderman. Night, night, Terry •130

One day we'll lose the Ashes and it will be as
horrific as waking up after a night on the drink in
a room full of images of Camilla Parker Bowles.

Sydney Morning Herald *before the 2005 Ashes; wonder what form their nightmares
took after the 2010-11 series — Shane Warne belly-dancing naked, anyone?* •131

We have put ourselves in a position of real strength and can push on to fulfil our goal of winning this series 5-0. *Matthew Hayden after Lord's Test, 2005* •132

I've seen nothing to make me change my 5-0 prediction. *Oh, Glen, Glen, what were you thinking of?* •133

Everyone talks about Harmison and Flintoff and then you get these two rabbits who come on and take three wickets each. *Australian coach John Buchanan clearly doesn't rate Ashley Giles and Simon Jones* •135

Just when Wimbledon was safely over, the England cricket team have set out to undo Tim Henman as a cause of national neurosis. *Simon Barnes' nerves jangle during the 2005 Ashes series* •136

49

An innings of neurotic violence, of eccentric watchfulness, of brainless impetuosity and incontinent savagery. It was an extraordinary innings, a masterpiece, and it secured the Ashes for England. *Simon Barnes in* The Times *on Kevin Pietersen's innings at the Oval in 2005* •137

This Test series has an epic grandeur capable of making all other big sporting events puny by comparison.

Michael Parkinson on the 2005 Ashes •138

Even in the dead of the Australian night, there is a palpable sense of England as a country alive again to the idiosyncratic, maddening, marvellous joys of cricket, indeed of a country reawakened to its sporting vocation.

Greg Baum of The Age *on the 2005 Ashes series* •139

I didn't know what to do when we won the Ashes. Thank God I didn't slide on my knees like a cheap medallion footballer.

Graeme Swann, the King of cricket tweeters •141

Goochie hadn't used it much and I thought there were a few runs left in it.

Ian Botham, on why he used Graham Gooch's bat for his momentous innings at Headingley, 1981. Gooch scored 2 and 0 •113

If I'd done a quarter of the things of which I'm accused, I'd be pickled in alcohol. I'd be a registered addict and would have sired half the children in the world's cricket-playing countries. *Ian Botham* •162

You should have stuck to soccer, lad.

Len Muncer, coach, to Ian Botham. Len who? •142

He's like a big soft puppy really.

Tom Cartwright on the young Ian Botham •143

He doesn't give a damn; he wants to ride
a horse, down a pint, roar around the land,
waking up the sleepers, show them things
can be done. As it is, he has to play cricket
all the time, and worry about
newspapermen, a Gulliver tied down
by the little people. *Peter Roebuck* •144

I don't think I've actually drunk a beer for fifteen years,
except a few Guinness's in Dublin, where it's the law.

Ian Botham, launching his own wine range •160

52

Ian Botham represents everything that's best in Britain. He's Biggles, the VC, El Alamein, the tank commander, he's everything. I mean, how could a schoolboy not want to be like Ian Botham?

Tim Hudson celebrates the nation's martial past •145

I'd rather face Dennis Lillee with a stick of rhubarb than go through all that again.

Ian Botham after his successful court battle to clear his name of assault •158

I think we have created a Frankenstein, bigger than life. *Maxi Hudson, Tim's wife, after the severance* •147

The first rock-and-roll cricketer.

Len Hutton on Botham, 1986 •148

If you made him Prime Minister tomorrow he'd pick this country up in ten minutes.

Umpire Bill Alley on Ian Botham •149

He lifted the game from a state of conventional excitement to one of unbelievable suspense and drama and finally into the realm of romantic fiction.

Henry Blofeld on Ian Botham •150

This fellow is the most overrated player I have ever seen. He looks too heavy, and the way he's been bowling out here, he wouldn't burst a paper bag.

Harold Larwood on Ian Botham •151

Botham? I could have bowled him out with a cabbage, with the outside leaves still on.

A bold as brass(ica) assessment from former Australian all-rounder and (later) umpire, Cec Pepper •152

Lillee will always be a better bowler than me.

Ian Botham, after breaking Dennis Lillee's Test wicket-taking record •153

Ian is a man who is very warm in friendship but very ugly in enmity.

Peter Roebuck on Botham, 1988 •154

Botham's biggest trick has been to convince people of his standing as an anti-establishment hero. Rarely has a cricketer been so protected by those in power. *Peter Roebuck* •155

He walked into the dressing-room and there's a lot of young guys in there, and he came up to me and said, "All right, Cat, how are you son?" and I thought, "Hold on a minute, this is good, I'm playing for England with fucking Ian Botham." *Phil Tufnell* •156

One may scoff at the idea of the Test match temperament, but it is a very real thing. The greatness of the occasion before now has accounted, I'll be bound, for almost as many failures as the greatness of the attack.

G.L. Jessop •163

I've heard it said that this game at Test level is fifty per cent in the mind, fifty per cent in the heart, and bugger technique, and that's not far off the mark.

Raymond Illingworth •164

It's Test cricket, it's tough. If you want an easy game, take up netball. *Steve Waugh* •165

Most people looking at the game from the outside cannot hope to appreciate the strain involved. Each test match is a week full of pressure. I notice it more when new players join the England side. Take Les Taylor — he is a very experienced cricketer, yet the transition to Test level took him by surprise. He felt a differenmce in the atmosphere and tension, and like all newcomers found himself drained of energy more quickly than usual. *David Gower, 1985.* •166

For thorough enjoyment, Test matches were too deadly serious. One always had the feeling of sitting on a barrel of gunpowder in contiguity to a lighted match and at the mercy of an untoward puff of wind.

G.L. Jessop •167

The public will no longer pay to stomach go-slow, draw-ridden Test stuff. *Cedric Rhoades, Lancashire chairman, after crowds dwindle for England v India series, 1971* •168

That must be the greatest heist since the Great Train Robbery. *Allan Border after Australia beat Sri Lanka despite a 291 run first innings deficit* •169

I'll tell you what pressure is. Pressure is a Messerschmitt up your arse. Playing cricket is not.

Keith Miller •170

It has not been Hick's fate to enjoy the fierceness of Test cricket. He was given almost all the characteristics demanded by greatness. Conviction alone was missing. *Peter Roebuck on Greme Hick,* Wisden 1999 •171

Intervals of whatever kind are, as every cricketer knows, the best of change bowlers.

Sir Jack Hobbs. **The Test Match Surprise** *(1926)* •172

If we speeded up between overs we'd beat you in three days instead of four.

Desmond Haynes not illogical defence of the West Indies' slow over rate in the 1980's •173

I do not know that Test cricket can be saved. I hope so but I am not convinced. People will no longer sit through five days of a match. Those days are long gone. People don't go to watch beautiful defensive shots or the battle of tactics any more. Unless something is done to change the rules and the manner in which it is played, then officials will have a hard time to make it attractive.

Lynton Taylor, Channel 9 executive,1978 •175

The refuse tip has been overflowing with talented but complex characters — Lewis, Ramprakash, Tufnell, Hick — who, with sensitive, imaginative handling could all have produced so much more. But no, we go on blindly stating that "If three lions on your chest doesn't motivate you, nothing will" and dismiss people with, "he's just a show-pony," without ever comprehending why they fail to deliver. I'll tell you why. Because they're all wracked with self-doubt. *Simon Hughes* •176

After all that Closey's only made a single!

John Edrich, after he and Brian Close took a pummelling from a pumped-up West indies attack in 1976. Close was 46 years old and black and blue.•177

In an England cricket eleven, the flesh may be of the South, but the bone is of the North, and the backbone is Yorkshire.
Len Hutton. To which we reply, Paul Jarvis •178

The only time an Australian walks
is when his car runs out of petrol.

Barry Richards •179

All we have to worry about now are
the future players who will have to face
being described as 'The Next Flintoff'.

*Peter Hayter,*Wisden, *2006* •180

If this bloke is a Test match bowler,
then my backside is a fire engine.

David Lloyd's unsual appraisal of Nathan Astle's bowling talents •181

On present form Waqar and Wasim could
bowl out the England team with an orange.

Geoff Boycott on the woes of 90's England •182

It's not as if they don't know what I am bowling, it's almost as if they don't really seem to care what I'm bowling.

Stuart MacGill after receiving some harsh punishment from the Indian batsmen in 2003 •183

I am not sure if such simulated training is going to be a help. You mean to say if we tour Australia we need to have a beer-can in our hands all the time?

Harbhajan Singh's response to New Zealand's preparation for India by reproducing the din inside the grounds during nets •184

I remember some good Saturdays against the West Indies before — the only trouble is that the Thursdays, Fridays, Mondays and Tuesdays were a bit of a disaster. *John Emburey* •185

Innovations invariably are suspect and in
no quarter more so than the cricket world.

Gilbert Jessop.•186

What is the good of an innings of fifty
if that man drops a couple of catches
and lets by forty or fifty runs. He has
not only wiped his own runs off the
slate, but he has probably upset the
bowlers into the bargain.

*AER Gilligan in an early appreciation
of decent fielding* •187

Cricket must be the only business
where you can make more money in
one day than you can in three. *Pat Gibson* •188

If there is a threat to the game of cricket, that
threat lies in the first-class arena. One-day cricket,
especially day-night, cricket, is here to stay.

Donald Bradman •189

The next thing you know, they'll be wanting to play with a ball with a bell in it.

Alec Bedser's response to Packer's introduction of floodlit matches. •194

Throw down some sawdust, everybody put on top hats and red noses, and you've got the John Player League.

Brian Close, 1969 •195

This game is injecting a dementia into the souls of those who play it.

Bill O'Reilly, Sydney Morning Herald *on effects of one-day cricket, 1982* •196

The dot ball has become the Holy Grail.

Colin Cowdrey, 1982 •197

For six days, thou shalt push up and down the line but on the seventh day thou shalt swipe.

Doug Padgett in the early days of the Sunday League •192

One-day cricket has debased the currency, both of great finishes and of adjectives to describe them.
Matthew Engel (1984) Reprinted in **The Guardian Book of Cricket** *(1986)* •199

A Test match is like a painting. A one-day match is like a Rolf Harris painting. *Ian Chappell* •200

We came to play cricket but lost at skittles.
Alan Igglesden after Kent lost a bowl-out in 1994 •201

You can see the moon. How far do you want to see?

Arthur Jepson, umpire, to Jack Bond in the famous Gillette Cup tie between Lancashire and Gloucestershire at Old Trafford in 1971. The game ended at 8.50pm •202

If I can see 'em, I can hit 'em.

David Hughes, just before scoring 24 off an over to settle the tie •203

You don't expect to be beaten by a tail-ender — not at midnight anyway.

Roger Knight finds it a bit hard to take •204

This may not have been cricket to the purists, but by golly it was just the stuff the doctor ordered.

Peter Wilson of the Daily Mirror *on the first Gillette Cup final* •205

Cricket has a nasty habit of punishing those who come to believe in their infallibility...

Malcolm Marhsall on WI defeat by India in the 1983 World Cup Final •206

I knew that God was on our side.

Imran Khan on beating England in the 1992 World Cup Final •207

One-day cricket is like fast food.
No one wants to cook. *Viv Richards* •216

There is a possibility that your ability as
a player may well be analysed by a future
generation on your one-day statistics.
That's the day I dread most. *Allan Border* •209

This was royalty on the toilet,
pants around their ankles.

Mike Selvey on Australia's defeat by Bangladesh in a one-day match, 2005 •210

Following England in this World Cup is a bit like
following Newcastle United — you never know what
you're going to get. One minute we're beating South
Africa, the next we're losing to Ireland and Bangladesh.

*Graeme Swann with an honest appraisal of England's
inconsistent form at the 2011 World Cup* •211

"Where have you been?" asked my wife when I came home just after 9pm. I told her I had "been watching cricket and listening to music." She said "Don't be silly."

Clement Freud on the aftermath of a Twenty20 match. **Wisden 2006** •217

One-day cricket is entertaining all right, but not entirely a sport. Once sport consciously tries to be entertaining, it sets off on the short but dangerous road that leads to the Worldwide Wrestling Federation. *Simon Barnes, 1997* •190

The Ashes in two and a half hours: it has all the dignity of the Monty Python Summarise Proust competition.

Simon Barnes in **The Times** *on the Twenty20 match between England and Australia, 2005* •214

The game is being forced to reinvent itself to cater for those with the attention span of a gnat.

Martin Johnson in the Daily Telegraph on Twenty20 •215

In real cricket, the player who has developed imagination and skill makes the game, but in the one-day match it is the other way round. The match dictates to the player.

Brian Close, 1970 •191

Touring abroad represents a whole new
challenge for an international cricketer;
as well as the opposition XI he has hostile
crowds, boredom, a new culture and — before
the advent of neutral umpires — some strange
officiating to contend with. More than a few
top class players have found runs or wickets
far harder to come by once they leave
their native shore.

Where the English
language is unspoken
there can be no
real cricket.
Neville Cardus •218

England is not ruined because sinewy brown men from a distant colony sometimes hit a ball further and oftener than we do. *JB Priestley* •219

At Peshawar I stayed with a cousin of Jardine. On the first morning we parted on the doorstep, I to play cricket, he to settle a tribal war.
Lionel, Lord Tennyson, describing a 1937/8 tour of India. •220

The history of Pakistani cricket is one of nepotism, inefficiency, corruption and constant bickering. *Imran Khan* •227

[They] have shown us once again that cricket can be and should be played with either obvious delight or communicable disappointment — a human game — which is a truth that lay long and deeply hidden in certain countries that should know better.
R.C. Robertson-Glasgow on the 1963 West Indies •222

Being the manager of a touring team is rather like being in charge of
a cemetery — lots of people underneath you, but no one listening.

Wes Hall, manager of numerous West Indies tours,
including the troublesome visit to England in 1995 •223

It has been noticed before in Indian cricket that
there is a tendency for those who might be expected
to give a lead at certain vital times to slip away into
a kind of nether world where they cannot be held

accountable. They render themselves incommunicado.
Edward Docker, History of Indian Cricket *(1976)* •224

Since the England players arrived on 31st October, India had the
assassination of its Prime Minister and a British diplomat twenty four
hours after he entertained us, thousands of deaths in communal
slaughter, the Bhopal disaster, the world's most elaborate democratic
exercise and a spy scandal. One morning in New Zealand the main
item on the morning news concerned a fisherman trying to land
a large marlin. *Matthew Engel,* the Guardian, *1985* •225

When I started playing in 1970, we used to improvise with maize cobs, using sticks as bats. We graduated to tennis balls and carved our own bats.

Steve Tikolo of Kenya, 1996, after they beat West Indies in the World Cup •228

The contrast between the civilian life of the ordinary Australian cricketer and his existence as a touring Test player is fantastic. I cannot think of one of my contemporaries who was fabulous enough to live at a decent hotel or travel a hundred miles in luxury. *Arthur Mailey* •230

I don't go along with the argument that the players are under too much pressure and spending too much time away from home. They want to make big money out of the game — well the only way to do so is to our and play. Players cannot expect to sit on their backsides and be paid just for being Test cricketers. They must work at their profession if that is the profession they want. *Bobby Simpson, former Australian captain, in* **Howzat, *1980*** •231

We had dined well at the Kimberley Club, and the old Boer told me not to drink too much of the milk. Unfortunately I had done so. The result was that in less time than it takes to relate, I was vomiting little pieces of iced milk, which made my throat so bad I couldn't speak for three days — shows we must take advice in strange countries.

Sammy Woods on Lord Hawke's tour to South Africa •232

You can't muck around with eggs and you can't muck around with chips. *Ken Barrington, explaining his eating habits in India, quoted in Frank Keating's* Another Bloody Day in Paradise, 1981 •233

I've done the elephant, I've done the poverty — I might as well go home. *Phil Tufnell on tour in India. (To be fair Tufnell was kidding; he wrote sensitively about the appalling poverty he saw out there)* •234

When I started touring I was like everyone else; hotel, a few beers in the bar, a simple life. Mike Whitney encouraged me to go out and have a look. *Steve Waugh on touring other lands* •235

73

A cricket tour in Australia would be the most delightful period in your life… if you were deaf.
Harold Larwood •236

Occupation: net bowler.

Jack Birkenshaw, England's third spinner on the 1972/73 tour to India, wrote this on his immigration card •238

Three to six months of constant packing and unpacking, living out of a suitcase with home a succession of impersonal hotel rooms, some good, some bad, the majority indifferent. The tourist's life is in the open, with every move made under the spotlight of publicity. *John Snow* •229

While they were in this place with gold tigers and everything there were crippled blokes on the street of Calcutta who couldn't even get anything to eat. It made me sick.
Phil Tufnell showed commendable social concern, if little tact towards the hosts, India, 1992-93 •240

It's 8.30 on a Friday night; what am I doing in Ahmedabad?

Graeme Fowler, England's tour of India 1984, in Vic Marks's Marks Out of Eleven, *1985* •241

You could feel each delivery
double declutch on pitching.

Colin Cowdrey on the slow Indian wickets, 1963/64 •242

I just want to get into the middle
and get the right sort of runs.

Robin Smith in India, after a bout of the dreaded Delhi belly •243

Cricket is a foreign game played in white flannels. It
is not our game, wrestling is. In fact, cricket should
not be played at all. What baffles me is why Indians
are so bothered about watching cricket.

*Mulayam Singh Nadav, Chief Minister in Uttar Pradesh, fails
to appreciate a national obsession* •244

An excitable kind of mob. *Phil Tufnell, on the Pakistanis, 1992* •245

Pakistan is the sort of place every
man should send his mother-in-law
to, for a month, all expenses paid.

Ian Botham, returning from England's 1984 tour •246

Why don't you send in your mother-in-law now? She couldn't do any worse.

Aamir Sohail remembers the remark after Botham gets a duck in the 1992 World Cup Final in Melbourne. •247

They find a ghost in everything — the air, the food, the hotels — and also mock our culture. I will not even wrap a fish in these tabloids.
Shakoor Rana, Pakistan umpire, gets one observation right •248

Lord Hawke, had he been asked about it, might have taken the same view as I do about having families on tour.
It is no more the place for them than a trench on the Somme.
John Woodcock sides with a turn of the century right-wing aristocrat •250

I have played my best cricket when I have been with my wife. If wives are accepted into the happy family, things will be very much better.

Alan Knott on women on tour, 1977 •251

The Authorities should consider that a cricketer is more likely to have a proper night's sleep with his wife in beside him, rather than a temporary stand-in and all the parallel gymnastics that would follow.
Lindsay Lamb, 1996 •252

One of the cricketers brought his girlfriend out.
It was an expensive trip and the gesture was both
endearingly kind, and touchingly generous.
It might, on reflection, have been even more kind
and touchingly generous had he brought his
wife instead. *Frances Edmonds,* **Another Bloody Tour** *(1986)* •253

Wives and families must never tour again
with players… there is little team spirit and
even less fight. Women and children come
first for these players who have families.
To hell with the pride of England seems
to be their motto. *Keith Miller, former Australian
all-rounder, in* **Daily Express,** *1975* •254

There was an urgent need to be cheery and
upbeat on that tour, but from the moment
he got on the team bus every morning, our
Raymond was moaning — about the traffic,
the weather, the hotel, the breakfast — it
was all so negative. *Dermot Reeve on Raymond Illingworth* •255

His public relations and relaxed, imperturbable style were ideal qualifications for the rigours imposed by a long overseas tour.

Denis Compton on MJK Smith •256

A banal bunch of louts.

Ian Wooldridge, Daily Mail, *1995, on* The Barmy Army •257

You are carrying all the prejudices of England. You are representing deep and paranoid urges, jingoistic sentiments you may prefer to distance yourself from. But it is unavoidable.

Mike Brearley, 1987 •258

It is a mistake to think that the game as it is played now is a super physical strain. The comforts are greater — hotels and travelling — the pay is doubled, the hours are less. It is difficult to find fault with a life so pleasant as is that of the county cricketer. **The Cricketer, 1931** •259

It is the bugbear of Yorkshiremen that they always feel that they have to behave like Yorkshiremen, or like their fixed belief in what a Yorkshireman should be: tough, ruthless, brave, mean.
Alan Gibson •286

As preparation for a Test Match, the domestic game is the equivalent of training for the Olympic marathon by taking the dog for a walk. *Martin Johnson, 1985* •261

Most of us were technically better at fourteen than we are now. *Peter Roebuck on the bad habits picked up playing county cricket* •262

Too much crap cricket on crap wickets.
Tom Moody with a blunt assessment of England's problems, 1997 •263

The rush of sponsorship in the early seventies did for English cricket, because it propped up the knackered counties and the weak players who should have been consigned to the history of the game. *Greg Chappell* •264

It's typical of English cricket. A tree gets in the way for 200 years and when it falls down, instead of cheering, they plant a new one.

Dave Gilbert has an unsentimental view of the great lime tree at Canterbury. He's Australian, by the way •265

They can all resign themselves to the fact that none of them will ever be quite as good as the talkative gentleman with the packet of ham sandwiches who sits square with the wicket on every county ground in the land. *Doug Insole, on the lot of a county Captain* •266

Tennesse Williams remains in America, which probably accounts for the fact that no dramatist has yet utilised the terrible frustrations of county captains as a vehicle for modern tragedy.

Doug Insole, **Cricket from the Middle *(1960)*** •267

Let him go then, and he can take any other bugger who feels t'same way.

Brian Sellers says goodbye to Ray Illingworth after contract negotiations founder •284

The vast majority of county cricketers have two topics of conversation: 'Me and My Cricket', or as high day and holiday variant, 'My Cricket and Me'. *Frances Edmonds, 1994* •276

The modern cricketer is not an ogre, nor is he deliberately obstructive. Although in most cases it would be unfair to dismiss him as a spoilt brat, he is too often lazy, ill-disciplined and reluctant to put in the effort and dedication commensurate with what he is earning. He has a very low boredom threshold with a constant need to be told what to do with his time. *Bob Willis, 1985* •277

When I left Yorkshire I received a letter from the secretary saying they were not going to offer me a contract which began: 'Dear Ray Illingworth', but the 'Ray' had been crossed out. They couldn't even bring themselves to call me by my first name or use a fresh piece of paper.

Ray Illingworth. •285

Sussex have always been regarded as the amateur gin-and-tonic men of English cricket — well, I'm going to change all that.

Tony Greig, 1974 •279

There never was a good skipper of a bad side. And I've got a great one. I could go out with any of them tonight just as easily as I could with my wife. *Jack Bond on Lancashire, 1972* •268

The Julie Andrews of cricket.

Peter Roebuck on former Sussex capatin John Barclay •269

During the winter I train on 20 fags and a couple of pints of lager and an unrelieved diet of cricket talk.
Brian Brain •270

Now that he's Derbyshire captain, he'll have to behave more like an adult than an overtired kid. *Devon Malcolm, 1998, on Dominic Cork* •271

Shall we put our heads down and make runs, or get out quickly and make history?
Don Shepherd joining Peter Walker with Glamorgan 11-8 v Leicestershire, 1971. •272

Something of the old pro attaches itself to Austin, something of the game as it was before fads, diets and personal counselling.
Michael Henderson on Ian Austin •273

When I first joined Middlesex there was a big card school, which would start up when it rained, with quite a lot of money going down. Now, with all the public schoolboys in the Middlesex team, they play Scrabble. *Mark Ramprakash on changing times (or a return to the old days) at Lord's* •274

Yorkshire cricket is particular. It dominates the characters rather than the characters dominating the county.

Peter Thomas, Yorkshire Cricketers 1839-1939 *(1973)* •281

Don't tell me his average or his top score at Trent Bridge. How many runs, how many wickets did he get against Yorkshire?

D.R. Jardine's standard for judging potential Test cricketers. •282

He may be good enough for England, but not for Yorkshire.

Brian Sellers on Johnny Wardle, after Yorkshire sacked the England player •283

Cricket in Yorkshire
is not as it is elsewhere.
It never has been.
The club has always
been a battleground
of warring factions.
Civil War is never far
below the surface of
Yorkshire cricket.

James P Coldham •287

Bowlers may rightly claim they win
matches, but it is batsmen the public
want to see. The grace of Frank Woolley
or David Gower, the thrilling power of
Viv Richards or the genius of Bradman
and Tendulkar; all had an aura and
a presence at the crease that captivated
and entranced their audience.

The margin of error between middle and
edge of a cricket bat is, after all, only two
inches. That is a truth which never
enters a batsman's mind when
he is in form; when he is off, it can
become an obsessive hazard.

John Arlott •288

85

A true batsman should in most of his strokes tell the truth about himself. *Sir Neville Cardus,* Cricket *(1930)* •289

Hard-wicket cricket is like chess — there is no element of chance in it, and only those who perfect themselves survive.

W.J. Edrich, Cricket Heritage *(1948)* •290

Professional coaching is a man trying to get you to keep your legs close together when other men had spent a lifetime trying to get them wider apart.

Rachel Heyhoe-Flint, former England women's captain •291

The cut was never a business stroke. *Wilfred Rhodes* •292

Others scored faster; hit the ball harder, more obviously murdered bowling. No one else, though, ever batted with more consummate skill.

John Arlott on Jack Hobbs •293

A snick by Jack Hobbs is a sort of disturbance of cosmic orderliness.

Sir Neville Cardus •294

Hobbs, who perpetually shunned the limelight and later turned down the opportunity to be England's first professional captain, was the definition of English self-deprecation.

Simon Hughes **And God Created Cricket** •295

Merely to see him lift or swing a bat at close quarters, to observe the flexing, tensing and relaxing of his grip on the handle was to perceive the profound sensitivity of his batting.

John Arlott, Jack Hobbs (1952) *reprinted in* **The Guardian Book of Cricket** *(1986)* •296

It were impossible to fault him. He got 'em on good 'uns, he got 'em on bad 'uns, he got 'em on sticky 'uns, he got 'em on t'mat, against South African googlers, and he got 'em all over t'world.

Wilfred Rhodes on Jack Hobbs •297

> Frank Woolley and Jack Hobbs… were far too modest to be anything but pros. Both were self-contained, and while their style of batting was consistent with amateurism, both realised, like the champion egg-laying hen, that if their product wasn't up to standard, the fact of wearing a crown wouldn't save their heads.
>
> *Arthur Mailey* •298

Easy to watch, difficult to bowl to, and impossible to write about. When you bowled to him, there weren't enough fielders; when you wrote about him, there weren't enough words.

R.C. Robertson-Glasgow on Frank Woolley •299

> There was an extraordinary negligence about his batting, as though his thoughts were elsewhere; but what terrible things he did to bowlers.
>
> *Michael Meyer on Frank Woolley,* **Summer Days** *(1981)* •300

His cricket is compounded of soft airs and flavours. And the very brevity of summer is in it… The brevity in Woolley's batting is a thing of pulse and spirit, not to be checked by clocks, but only to be apprehended by imagination.
Neville Cardus on Frank Woolley, **Autobiography *(1947)*** •301

He carried, at all times, wherever he went, the hopes of the black, English-speaking Caribbean man.

Michael Manley on George Headley, **A History of West Indies Cricket *(1988)*** •302

For Hammond was majesty and power; Hammond was grace and beauty and courage. One glorious cover-drive from him and I would be content.
Margaret Hughes, **All on a Summer's Day *(1953)*** •303

The greatest player we shall ever see — but a funny bugger.
Wally Hammond, as seen by a Gloucestershire team-mate •304

I'm going while you still ask why. I'm not waiting until you ask why not.
Patsy Hendren, Middlesex and England batsman, explaining why he was retiring •305

Come and see this. Don't miss a minute of it. You'll never see the likes of this again.

Don Bradman to Australian side during Stan McCabe's 232 v England at Trent Bridge, 1938 •306

I never much enjoyed watching Hutton bat. I was always scared he might get out, just as mother was always scared what might happen to the best china if she took it out of the cabinet. *Alan Gibson,* Growing Up with Cricket *(1985)* •307

There's nothing we can teach this lad.

George Hirst, Yorkshire coach, on Hutton's first appearance at county nets, 1930 •308

Hutton has never given the public any cosy human view of himself which will allow them to recognise him as... capable... of the same errors of nerve and judgment as themselves.

J.M. Kilburn on Len Hutton •309

If there were 22 Trevor Baileys playing in a match, who would ever go and watch it? *Arthur Morris* •310

It requires an earthquake to make him change his game in midstream.

Doug Insole on Trevor Bailey, Cricket From The Middle *(1960)* •311

Edrich's batting was always a thing of guts and belligerence; watching him facing a fast bowler was like watching some unexpectedly tough little kid walking up to the school bully and kicking him smartly in the shins. *Barry Norman on Bill Edrich,*
County Champions *(1982)* •312

91

Dear Mr Edrich, I would like you to know that if
I did want to have all my teeth extracted in one go,
that is the way I wanted it done. Well played sir.

Letter from a Times *reader marvelling at Edrich hooking Harold Larwood* •313

In the country of the blind, the one-eyed man is
king. But in the keen-eyed world of cricket, a fellow
with just one good eye and a bit has to settle for
something less than the perfection he once sought.

The Nawab of Pataundi who continued playing cricket with only one good eye •314

I remember little about early coaching. I did not like nets.
I never did like them subsequently. I would use a net if I
wanted to correct a fault or was out of form. Otherwise, is
seemed to me that it encouraged a looseness of method
which would be found out in competitive cricket.

Peter May, A Game Enjoyed *(1985)* •315

He is the only athlete I have ever known who,
as he walked, sagged at ankles, knees and hips.

John Arlott on Ken Mackay, The Cricketer *(1963)* •316

His square-cut was like the quick fall
of a headsman's axe, clean and true.

Margaret Hughes on Cyril Washbrook, **All on a Summer's Day** *(1953)* •317

The cover drive is the most beautiful stroke
in cricket. Does that throw any light on why
I am a self-admitted lover of all things British
and traditional? *Colin Cowdrey. Not really.* •318

The name of Cowdrey is synonymous
with friendliness, charm, good manners,
modesty and other related virtues you
can think of, all underpinned by his
religious beliefs. *Gerry Cotter,* **The Ashes Captains** *(1989)* •319

He was the players' man, both spiritual and temporal.

Frank Keating, **Ken Barrington** *(1981), reprinted in the* **Guardian Book of Cricket** *(1986)* •320

93

Whenever I see Ken coming to the wicket, I imagine the Union Jack fluttering behind him.

Wally Grout, Australian wicketkeeper, 1965, on Ken Barrington, a renowned scrapper •321

They say the fool of the family always goes into the church.

Ted Dexter referring to a series of run-out disasters involving Rev. David Sheppard, Australia v England, 1963 •322

We were never coached. We used to practise in the streets of Signal Hill, where some of us would be hauled off to jail by the police if we were caught playing on the road. It was on one of these streets that I learned to play fast bowling.

Basil D'Oliveira, Time To Declare *(1980)* •323

He appeals to the aesthetic sense because of the innate elegance of his movement, the sensitivity with which he harnesses the ball's course, such a princely style as makes the batting of some Test players seem workaday stuff.

John Arlott on Barry Richards, Book of Cricketers *(1979)* •324

In spite of the maturity of his cricket, he was, at heart, still a small boy playing games.

Tony Lewis on Majid Khan, **Playing Days (1985)** •325

You don't need footwork in batting, just hands and eye.

Majid Khan to Glamorgan team-mates, 1969 •326

The stroke of a man knocking a thistle top off with a walking stick.

John Arlott admires a contemptuous pull-stroke from Clive Lloyd •327

I can't really say I'm batting badly. I'm not batting long enough to be batting badly.

Greg Chappell is philosophical about a bad trot •328

95

Perhaps it is best to say that, if all living things in India are incarnations, Gavaskar is technical orthodoxy made flesh. *Scyld Berry, 1983* •329

When you have two workhorses and shoot them in the back, I think it's evil. You don't treat animals in this way. I was blindfolded, led up an alley and assassinated.

Viv Richards, on being sacked by Somerset in 1986 •330

He is a fallible genius. He flirts with the record book when, we suspect, he could monopolise it. His cricket, always potent and often pure, is unwaveringly instinctive.

David Foot, Viv Richards *(1979)* •331

Proud as a peacock, handsome as a prince, strong as a horse, Viv Richards was for the best part of ten years recognised as the best batsman in the world. That is a big statement.

Christopher Martin-Jenkins, Cricket Characters *(1987)* •332

He is built like a guardsman and that expressionless face with the black moustache surely saw service in England's imperial wars, defending Rorke's Drift and marching up the Khyber Pass.

> *Travel writer Geoffrey Moorhouse waxes*
> *lyrical about Graham Gooch* •333

Gooch was honest and humble. He could be mournful. But he was never half-hearted.

> *Peter Roebuck* •334

I know I look a totally miserable sod on television. I wish I didn't. But there you are.

Graham Gooch is resigned to his natural expression •335

...is vaguely reminiscent of a shire horse. Strong, sturdy, reliable, unflappable.

> *Frances Edmonds on Mike Gatting,* **Another Bloody Tour** *(1986)* •336

One of the few men you would back to get past a Lord's gateman with nothing more than an icy stare.

Martin Johnson of Peter Willey •337

He has tended to symbolise the strengths and the defects of our batting in recent years – exotic strokeplay mixed up with suicidal tendencies.

Imran Khan on Javed Miandad, **Imran (1983)** •338

Border is a walnut. Hard to crack and without much to please the eye.

Peter Roebuck on Allan Border •339

You can see by his walk to the wicket, like a terrier out for a walk in a neighbourhood bristling with bigger dogs, that he is ready for a fight and not afraid of his ability to look after himself.

Christopher Martin-Jenkins on Alan Border, **Cricket Characters (1987)** •340

Look at Border. He's scored 10,000 Test runs and he's only got three shots — the cut, the cover drive and the pull.

Jack Birkenshaw pays Alan Border a back-handed compliment •341

Hick is just a flat-track bully.

John Bracewell coins a phrase that will stick with Graeme Hick in 1991 •342

At times he looks as though he has an artificial brain, slightly out of tune with his body.

Christopher Martin-Jenkins. C.M-J is too old school simply to suggest Hick isn't the brightest •343

Boon appears a most contented cricketer. I can visualise him on a sheep farm in Tasmania, sipping lager on the veranda, the ideal temperament for dealing with fast bowlers. *Sir Len Hutton, 1985* •344

Martin cultivates that class thing with his talk about wine and fine restaurants. It irritates the hell out of everybody outside Auckland.

John Bracewell on Martin Crowe •345

He won't be great until he stops being a perfectionist.

Ian Botham on Martin Crowe •346

The realisation that time is tapping you on the shoulder doesn't creep up on you, it literally swamps you overnight.

Mike Atherton on calling it a day •347

He was my first England captain, my first England opening partner, he stands next to me and bores the pants off me at slip — he's a great guy. *Mark Butcher on Mike Atherton* •348

One of the few men capable of looking more dishevelled at the start of a six-hour century than at the end of it.

Martin Johnson on Mike Atherton •349

Never sacrifice a strength to a compromise.

Alex Stewart explains a preference for opening the batting than keeping wicket •351

I'm an instinctive player but at the moment I'm thinking too much and have become a gibbering wreck.

1994, and Robin Smith becomes the latest to utter the standard cry of an out of form batsman •352

I don't suppose I can call you a lucky bleeder when you've got 347.

Angus Fraser sneaks one past the outside edge during Brian Lara's marathon 375 in 1994 •353

I don't think a better player could have broken the record. To me, Lara is the only batsman playing today who plays the game the way it should be played. He hits the ball with the bat, not the pad. *Gary Sobers gets a bit carried away* •354

I still have the butterflies, but now I have them flying in formation.

Mark Taylor on getting out of a rut of bad form •355

He just emanates joy, the kind of joy that comes from somebody who is filled with the Holy Spirit.

Hansie Cronje on Jonty Rhodes •356

Being a Christian does not mean that you have to stand down from a conflict. God does not want me to be second best. *Jonty Rhodes* •357

Inzamam-ul-Haq's languid batting can make Marcus Trescothick's footwork seem like a qualification for a starring role in Riverdance. *Mike Selvey on Inzamam-ul-Haq* •358

I'd be out the back with a cricket ball in a sock three or four hours on end just hitting through the roof. I loved it and thought this was all there was in the world. *Steve Waugh* •359

He brought more to the game than just his cricket. When you think of Steve Waugh, you think of toughness, competitiveness, positiveness, never giving up, of that Anzac spirit.
Kim Hughes on Steve Waugh •360

Steve Waugh's career has been filled with the kind of heroic innings most talented players would have been proud to play just once, let alone to order. Like some immutable law of physics, Waugh has always saved his best for the most unpromising situations.

Derek Pringle on Steve Waugh •361

He was unstoppable. I'll be going to bed having a nightmare of Sachin just running down the wicket and belting me for six. I don't think anyone, besides Don Bradman is in the same class.

Shane Warne on Sachin Tendulkar, 1998 •362

Batsmen walk out into the middle alone. Not Tendulkar. Every time Tendulkar walks to the crease a whole nation, tatters and all, march with him to the battle arena. A pauper people, pleading for relief, remission from the lifelong anxiety of being Indian, by joining in spirit their visored saviour.

Indian poet C.P. Surendran, quoted in And God Created Cricket by Simon Hughes (2009) •363

You think there are only so many times that Laxman can run down the wicket and hit you through the onside if the ball is turning out of the rough. Then 280 runs later he hasn't mistimed one and you wonder if you should try something different.

Shane Warne on bowling to Australia's nemesis, 2001 •364

He walks out to bat radiating as much intensity as someone toddling to the newsagent for the *Racing Post*. *Gideon Haigh on the easy-going Damien Martyn* •365

Sometimes I wish I was Adam Gilchrist.

New Zealand plodder, Mark Richardson, after a six-hour 93 •366

Ed Smith disguised any nerves with such quintessential English charm that one observer wondered whether Hugh Grant had been drafted into the squad.

Richard Hobson, The Times, *2003* •367

Few of the great players are deep theorists on cricket, probably because the game has come to them too naturally to need any very close analysis. *E.W. Swanton,* Denis Compton: A Cricket Sketch *(1948)* •368

Enjoyment given and felt, is the chief thing about Compton's batting. It is a clear-flowing stream, a breath of half-holiday among work days.

R.C. Robertson-Glasgow •369

Compton belonged in the Golden Age. He had the same adventurous spirit as the top batsmen of that time.

E.M. Wellings, Vintage Cricketers *(1983)* •370

I wouldn't say I coached him, but I didn't mess him up.

George Fenner, head coach at Lord's, on his early coaching of Compton, 1958 •371

I was as fit as a flea; I did what came naturally and I enjoyed myself.

*Denis Compton's recollection of his vintage 1947 season,
which brought 3816 first-class runs and 18 centuries* •372

I doubt if one in a hundred understood what they were really watching was total batsman-domination of mediocre bowling.

*Colin Cowdrey, offering a less romanticized judgment
of the same summer, immediately after the end of
WW2, of flat pitches and depleted attacks.* •373

How much simpler it is to swat a fly with a rolled-up newspaper than with a telephone directory.

Denis Compton, not a fan of heavy bats •374

If Mohammed Ali can sway inside a straight left from three feet, I'm sure that Brearley can avoid a bouncer from 22 yards. *Denis Compton, not a fan of helmets* •375

I hate the helmets, the visors and the chest protectors, I would dearly love the boys to go out there like playboys, with a box, some gloves and a bat, play off the back foot and enjoy it.

Denis Compton, not a fan of common sense •376

I couldn't bat for the length of time required
to score 500. I'd get bored and fall over.
Denis Compton, 1994 •377

Even the most misanthropic critic must succumb
to the smacking concussion of the full-blooded
hit, to the fascination of the red ball rocketing
into the blue sky, with its whirring flight of a
driven partridge and its final crash as it lands on
roof or window. *Hon. T.C.F. Prittie,* **Mainly Middlesex *(1947)*** •378

Pietersen would be deemed brash
by a Texan assertiveness coach.
Simon Wilde on Kevin Pietersen, **Sunday Times** •412

Jessop was a terror. We reckoned in one game we'd
make him go and fetch 'em. So we bowled wide on the
offside. He fetched 'em all right. He went off like a
spring trap and, before you'd seen his feet move, he was
standing at the offside of his stumps, pulling 'em over
the square leg boundary. *Wilfred Rhodes* •379

There was no swagger: just a huge relish for the confrontation, and an inner certainty about his newly acquired greatness.

Simon Barnes on Andrew Flintoff, Wisden 2006 •406

Nerves play as important a part in batsmanship as skill.

Gilbert Jessop •381

The batsman who does nearly everything a batsman ought not to do — with consummate success. The insolent unorthodoxy of his methods and the combined frequency and power of his hitting mark him as truly unique.

C.B.Fry & G.W.Beldam on Gilbert Jessop in Great Batsmen (1905) •382

Crouch he certainly did, for style meant nothing to him. Batting was a glorious gamble.

A.G.Moyes on Gilbert Jessop, known as The Croucher for his exaggerated stance, in A Century of Cricketers (1950) •383

His speed of foot and eye and judgement, his strength
of wrist, his timing and daring, all made him the most
dangerous batsman the world will ever see; he didn't go
in for huge hits; he made boundaries out of balls that the
best batsman would be content just to play.

S.M.J. Woods, The Cricketer, *on G.L. Jessop* •384

On the leg-side of the wicket lay safety; on the off the surgery
windows. Small wonder, therefore, if a pronounced penchant for
the 'pull' should have affected my batting throughout my days.

*G.L. Jessop on cricket at home in a small garden with
attendant punishment for breaking his father's window* •385

Vegetarianism may be cure for all the ills which flesh is
heir to, but it is wretched stuff to make runs on. For the
whole month of May I could get neither runs nor wickets.

G.L. Jessop on his poor form in may 1898 after an attack of renal colic •386

The 'Old Man' (W.G.) was much concerned over my ill success,
and resolved to prescribe for me in his own fashion. I forgot whether
it was Goelet 1889 or Moet 1886… anyway it had the desired effect,
and I bade farewell to vegetarianism for ever.
G.L. Jessop on his return to form. •387

There are many cries for the batsman to get behind the ball, but how can you hit it hard if you are behind it? *Ted Dexter* •391

Fender gave some amusement by hitting Armstrong back-handed on the offside for a couple.

Pelham Warner in 1921. Was this the first reverse sweep? •389

It's hard work making batting look effortless. *David Gower* •400

I never wanted to make a hundred. Who wants to make a hundred anyway? When I first went in, my immediate objective was to hit the ball to each of the four corners of the field. After that I tried not to be repetitive.

Sir Learie Constantine, speech to Royal Commonwealth Society, 1963 •390

This is the first time in the last ten years that I've played a maiden over.

Virender Sehwag, not known for slow scoring, is shocked after six dot balls from Lalith Malinga •410

112

He remains a laid-back charming goldilocks with a touch
of genius at the crease, no histrionic tactics or tantrums
in the field, an ambassadorial approach to the world.
Frank Keating on David Gower, **The Guardian Book of Cricket** *(1986)* •401

I suppose I can gain some consolation from the fact
that my name will be permanently in the record books.
Malcolm Nash, Glamorgan bowler, after being hit for six sixes by Gary Sobers •392

It was not sheer slogging through
strength, but scientific hitting with
every movement working in harmony.
Tony Lewis, Glamorgan captain, on those six sixes •393

John Kennedy once wrote of courage as 'grace,
under pressure'. Sobers had all of that but under
pressure he had something else: the capacity to
counterattack and to direct his riposte to the
precise requirement of the situation.
Michael Manley, **A History of West Indies Cricket** *(1988)* •394

Ricky Ponting looks like how I would imagine Jimmy Krankie
would've turned out with the aid of human growth hormones.
TV presenter Gabby Logan on the (then) Australian captain •411

113

The greatest all-round player the world has ever seen, he was happy to stand or fall by his belief that cricket, even at Test level, should be entertaining.

Ray Illingworth on Gary Sobers, Captaincy *(1980)* •395

For him, cricket was a way of making a lot of friends, knocking the cover off the ball if possible and making regular attempts to boost the profits of various breweries.

Mike Procter on Gloucestershire colleague, David Green, 1981 •396

Perhaps Gower will eventually realise that cricket's not always about champagne. It's a bread-and-butter game.

Brian Brain, a bread-and-butter cricketer •397

Gower might have been more at home in the 1920s or 1930s, cracking a dashing hundred for MCC, the darling of the crowds, before speeding away in a Bugatti and cravat for a night on the town.

Scyld Berry •398

Difficult to be more laid back without being actually comatose.

Frances Edmonds on David Gower •399

As far as I'm concerned I'm just having fun,
playing cricket with my mates.
Andrew Flintoff, 2005 •405

> That means I can drive a flock of sheep through the town
> centre, drink for free in no less than 64 pubs, and get a lift
> home with a policemen when I become inebriated. What
> more could you want? *Andrew Flintoff, freeman of Preston* •407

Having been floored by a bouncer he stood up, doffed his cap and made an
exaggerated bow to the bowler. After swaying out of thye way of another he
performed a backward somersault. Fussing and fidgeting at the crease, and
constantly talking to himself, some of his innings were pure slapstick.

Simon Hughes in **And God Created Cricket** *on the idiosyncracies*
of Derk Randall's memorable innings in the Centenary Test•402

He's a once-in-a-generation cricketer.

Steve Waugh on Adam Gilchrist •403

> This was combustible stroke play that challenged our
> assumptions. Steady starts, playing yourself in, wickets
> in hand — such tenets had been adapted for sure, to the
> demands of one-day cricket, but never so freely abandoned.
> Jayasuriya's method of playing himself in seemed to
> consist of taking three steps down the pitch and
> carving the ball high over cover.
> **Wisden on Sanath Jayasuriya** •404

Mandela's first words to me were: Fraser, can you please tell me, is Donald Bradman still alive?

Malcolm Fraser, PM of Australia at the time of Mandela's release •413

A coach who suppresses natural instincts may find that he has lifted a poor player to a mediocre one but has reduced a potential genius to the rank and file. *Don Bradman* •414

Figures are not entirely conclusive, especially short-term figures, but it is difficult to avoid their significance if a man produces them year after year against every type of opponent and under all conceivable conditions. *Sir Donald Bradman, Farewell to Cricket (1950)* •415

I saw him playing on television and was struck by his technique,
so I asked my wife to come look at him. Now I never saw myself play,
but I feel that this player is playing much the same as I used to play, and
she looked at him on television and said yes, there is a similarity
between the two... his compactness, technique, stroke production...
it all seemed to gel. *The Don recognises a chip off the old block
in Sachin Tendulkar* •416

Promise there is in Bradman in plenty, though watching him
does not inspire one with any confidence that he desires to take
the only course which will lead him to a fulfilment of that promise.
He seems to live for the exuberance of the moment.
P.G.H. Fender on the young Don, **The Turn of the Wheel** *(1929)* •417

No bigger than a cloud the size of a man's hand when he first
appeared, he was destined to plague and dominate our bowlers
for nearly a quarter of a century, and to write his name in very
big letters in the chronicles of the game.
Sir Pelham Warner, **Long Innings** *(1951)* •418

If genius is the art of doing the simple things properly
Bradman was a classic example. Whilst lesser players tend to
create complications, or theorise themselves towards a state
of mental exhaustion, Bradman knew precisely what he
intended to do, and went his way with the minimum of fuss.
Alec Bedser, **Cricket Choice** *(1981)* •419

117

Bradman was a team in himself. I think the Don was too good: he spoilt the game. He got too many runs. The pot calling the kettle black? No, I was human; he got hundreds every time he went in… He was mechanical; he was the greatest run-getting machine of all-time. I do not think we want to see another one quite like him. I do not think we ever shall. *Jack Hobbs,* **The Times, 1952** •420

Bradman was the summing up of the Efficient Age which succeeded the Golden Age. Here was brilliance safe and sure, streamlined and without impulse. Victor Trumper was the flying bird; Bradman the aeroplane.

Neville Cardus, **Autobiography (1947)** •421

How to get Bradman out is developing into a pastime for rainy days.

Arthur Mailey •422

Pin him down! Of course not! I bowled every ball to get the little devil out. *Maurice Tate, England bowler* •423

The bowler who is confronted by Bradman and doesn't think, doesn't bowl for long.

Harold Larwood, England fast bowler •424

Bradman didn't break my heart in 1930, he just made me very, very tired. *Harold Larwood* •425

The Don had two views of bouncers — one when they were bowled against him and the other when bowled by his side with no fear of retaliation. *Jack Fingleton, after Bradman's team (including Lindwall and Miller) peppered sides with bouncers after the war* •426

If someone had produced a batting helmet during the Bodyline series, I would certainly have worn it.

Donald Bradman •427

A number of Bradmans would quickly put an end to the glorious uncertainty of cricket. *Neville Cardus* •428

It's not easy to bat with tears in your eyes.

Don Bradman, on his final Test innings in 1948 •429

Crowds have always been thrilled by a combination of athleticism and testosterone and the whiff of battle and this is what fast bowlers give to cricket. The gladiatorial nature of a contest between a fast bowler in full cry and a top batsman refusing to yield remains one of the cornerstones of cricket's appeal.

Facing a fast bowler is like standing on the outside lane of the M1, and when the car is 22 yards away, trying to get out of the way.

Alec Stewart •430

121

None of us likes fast bowling, but some of us don't let on.
Maurice Leyland •431

There is a final drop of venom
which transforms a good bowler
into a great one. *TCF Prittie* •432

Korty matched his furious speed with a furious
temper. He took strong personal dislikes to batsmen
and revelled in the guise of the terrifying paceman.
Charles Sale on CK Kortright, **Korty** *(1986)* •433

The secret of bowling is rhythm, and all who
achieve high speed know of those magical days
when everything clicks that much more smoothly.
E W Swanton, 'Gubby' Allen *(1985)* •434

I used to give every new batsman four balls, One was a bouncer to check his courage, the second a fizzer to check his eyesight, the third was a slow 'un to try out his reflexes and the fourth a bender to see if he was a good cricketer. And if he took a single off each of the four balls, I knew I was in trouble. *Harold Larwood* •435

He was, for a certainty, the only bowler who quelled Bradman; the only bowler who made Bradman lose his poise and balance, departing from his set path of easeful centuries into flurried and agitated movements.

Jack Fingleton on Harold Larwood, **Brightly Fades the Don** *(1949)* •436

How he ever stood the strain of bowling at such terrific speed match after match I don't know. It was amazing. *Sir Donald Bradman on Harold Larwood,* **My Cricketing Life** *(1938)* •437

123

There's no sitting duck like a scared duck. *Ray Lindwall* •438

In the art of fast bowling Ray Lindwall has no peer. To me he was the greatest of them all.

Fred Trueman, From Larwood to Lillee *(1983)* •439

He was a great man at a party, and played his part in ensuring that no English brewery went out of business through lack of patronage.

Jim Laker on Ray Lindwall, Over to Me *(1960)* •440

I shouldn't have done that.

Ray Lindwall upon hitting Tyson with a bouncer during the Australia v England series, 1954/5. •441

For young boys he was something out of Boys' Own Paper, the one cricketer likely to sustain fantasy.
Mihir Bose, Keith Miller *(1979)* •442

Fred Trueman the mature fast bowler was a sharply pointed and astutely directed weapon; Fred Trueman the man has often been tactless, haphazard, crude, a creature of impulse.
John Arlott, in Fred *(1971)* •443

People started calling me Fiery because Fiery rhymes with Fred, just like Typhoon rhymes with Tyson.

Trueman on poetry •444

Some men have bowled a cricket ball faster than Trueman, but none has done so with more gusto. As much as anything his triumphs have been based on sheer belligerence. *Geoffrey Moorhouse,* Fred Trueman *(1956) reprinted in* The Guardian Book of Cricket *(1986)* •445

Without rival, the ripest, the richest, the rip-roaringest
individual performer on cricket's stage.
A.A. Thomson, **The Cricketer,** *1961, on Freddie Trueman.* •446

Fred Trueman was the kind of fast bowler he had
created for himself; a larger-than-life sized figure
compounded in the imagination of the boy from
the fancies, facts, loyalties, cricket, reading,
traditions and all other influences of a semi-rural,
semi industrial area of South Yorkshire in the 1930s.
John Arlott, in **Fred,** *1971* •447

To bowl fast is to revel in the glad animal action, to thrill
in physical power and to enjoy a certain sneaking feeling of
superiority over the mortals who play the game. *Frank Tyson* •448

Frank Tyson brings back the days of the
demon bowler to cricket. By sheer speed
he subdues batsmen, splinters stumps,
silences barrackers, sways Test rubbers.
Ray Robinson, **The Glad Season** *(1955)* •449

126

A fag, a cough, a cup of coffee.

Brian Statham, Lancashire and England seam bowler on his pre-match breakfast. •450

Neither of us worried who got the wickets
as long as we were in our favourite position
— our feet up, watching England bat.

Brian Statham, Fred Trueman's strike partner for England •451

His temperament when bowling was also in keeping with
the 'spaghetti western' anti-hero — mean, moody and
essentially a loner who was permanently at odds with
the establishment, sometimes with, but often without
a cause. *Trevor Bailey on John Snow,* From Larwood to Lillee *(1983)* •452

I don't want any bloody sympathy do you
understand that? It has happened. People say
'I know how you feel' are just talking bullshit.
They don't know, not at all. What I can't forget
is that the ball was a deliberate short one. Not
deliberately at his head, but still deliberate.

*Peter Lever, England fast bowler, after almost killing
New Zealand tail-ender, Ewen Chatfield* •453

I hate bowling at you. I'm not as good at hitting a moving target.

Dennis Lillee to the great fidget, Derek Randall •454

No good hitting me there mate, nothing to damage.

Derek Randall, responding to being 'skulled' by Dennis Lillee in Centenary Test, Melbourne, 1977 •455

I know I'm a ruthless bastard and I'll always have a go. But I wouldn't deliberately put a ball like that on anybody. It slipped. It honestly slipped.

Dennis Lillee, after bowling a beamer at Bob Willis in Sydney, Australia v MCC, 1974/5 •456

There's no batsman on earth who goes out to meet Dennis Lillee and Jeff Thomson with a smile on his face. *Clive Lloyd* •457

Cricket has given Lillee the prestige of a matinee idol and financial security for life, and he has had to work tremendously hard for them.

Jack Pollard, Australian Cricket *(1982)* •458

Good Lord, he's knocked old George off his horse now.

Geoff Arnold, watching from England's dressing room, as Dennis Lillee hit Keith Fletcher on the crest of his touring cap, MCC in Australia, 1974/5 •459

Well his mother was an actress, you know.
Mike Brearley on Mark Nicholas' theatrics after a Wayne Daniel bouncer •460

A 1914 biplane tied up with elastic bands vainly trying to take off.

Frank Keating on Bob Willis •461

Remember what happened to Graham Dilley, who started out as a genuinely quick bowler? They started stuffing line and length into his ear, and now he has Dennis Lillee's action with Dennis Thatcher's pace.

Geoff Boycott on the perils of coaching •462

There's nothing like the sound of flesh on leather to get a cricket match going.

Geoff Lawson thinks of Rollerball *during the 2005 Ashes* •463

He looks like a cuddly little panda.

England manager, Tony Brown's unsympathetic view of Mike Gatting after Malcolm Marshall's nose job bouncer •464

Rather like facing up to a raging bull. The refined run-up still has a disconcerting chicane in it, there is a lot of puffing and blowing, a grimace or two, a huge leap and some serious pace to follow.

Simon Hughes on Syd Lawrence •465

Q: What's your favourite animal.
Waugh: Merv Hughes

Steve Waugh in flippant mode in a
magazine questionnaire •466

Wickets are more important than waistline.
Merv Hughes •467

The mincing run-up resembles someone in high heels and a panty girdle chasing a bus.

Martin Johnson on Merv Hughes •468

You guys are history. You're going to pay for it.

Devon Malcolm gets hit by a bouncer and suggests the South Africans
would regret it. They did. He took 9-57 in the next innings •469

Sometimes it takes him a fortnight to put on his socks.

Mickey Stewart on Devon Malcolm •470

He tried to bowl the way they wanted him to bowl and hit the side of the net. At gnat's pace. Then he went back to bowling his old style and he bowled fast and swung it. *Graham Thorpe on attempts to re-model Devon Malcolm's action* •471

I knew I could dismiss Graeme Hick virtually any time I wanted.

Waqar Younis in 1996. Immodest, but essentially true •472

You don't need a helmet facing Waqar so much as a steel toe cap.

Simon Hughes on Waqar Younis' preference for fast swinging yorkers rather than a bouncer •473

132

Get a single down the other end and let someone else play him.

Geoff Boycott's advice on how to deal with Glenn McGrath •474

I just try to bore the batsmen out. It's pretty simple stuff but the complicated thing is to keep it simple.

Glen McGrath •475

I would love to bowl at 100 miles per hour. I like to see fear in a batsman. *Shoaib Akhtar* •476

A bloke's bowling at 150kmh trying to rip the fingers off your arms or probably even worse. It gets your blood going and the adrenalin pumping. You are in a fight. And to me that's what Test cricket is all about.

Justin Langer on facing Shoaib Akhtar •477

My grandfather would probably have slaughtered a cow in celebration if he'd been alive. *Makhaya Ntini, after a 5-for against England in 2003* •478

He's big and rawboned and I suspect he has the IQ of an empty swimming pool.

Adam Parore on Andre Nel of South Africa •479

This is a nice challenge, but when you look down at your shirt, that badge isn't there.

Steve Harmison sees through the PR-oriented Super Test •480

Fast bowlers are bully boys. They dish it out but they can't take it.

Brian Close •481

The first West Indian cricketers caught the imagination of the cricketing publics of England and Australia because they brought to the game a free-moving, free-stroking, lithe athleticism which was all their own. *Michael Manley,* **A History of West Indies Cricket** *(1988)* •482

If the West Indies are on top, they're magnificent. If they are down they grovel. And with the help of Brian Close and a few others, I intend to make them grovel.

Tong Greig, 1975. Oh dear •483

Wes Hall's personality was such that no one, not even the batsmen whom he bombarded, could take exception to him.

David Frith, **The Fast Men** *(1975)* •484

We have a saying in the West Indies — if you want to drive, buy a car.

Michael Holding eschews the good length ball •485

If I was bowling against this England team, I'd get a lot more Test wickets than I did; they're bloody scared.

Charlie Griffith, former West Indian pace bowler,
during England's tour of Caribbean, 1981 •486

The full implications of the religious teaching may have passed me by, but there was one overriding compensation which made those three hours absolutely compulsory. We played cricket. Needless to say, I never missed Sunday School, bible in one hand and cricket ball in the other.

Malcolm Marshall, Marshall Arts *(1987)* •487

I don't believe in leaping. No matter how high you jump, you have to come down.

Michael Holding keeps his feet on the ground •488

I don't know why they bother to put the stumps out. None of those buggers are trying to hit them.

Graeme Fowler, on the West Indian fast bowlers, 1985 •489

I was interested to hear Michael Holding say that Curtly is still learning. I hope he doesn't learn too much more. *Allan Border on Curtly Ambrose, 1983* •490

For one hour, on an untrustworthy pitch, he performed like the very devil himself.

Mark Nicholas describes Curtly Ambrose bowling England out for 46 in 1994 •491

Lloyd did more than employ four fast bowlers. He trained and moulded his players into the most awesome fielding side in history. *Michael Manley,* **A History of West Indies Cricket *(1988)*** •493

In their disregard of anybody being hurt and hit some West Indians appeared callous and reminded me of bully boys. *Jack Fingleton, 1980. Not like good old Thommo, eh Jack?* •494

If every country had an attack like the West Indies, Test cricket would die pretty quickly. You can only think of survival, not playing shots.

Allan Border joins in, 1989 •496

I once got an unplayable ball from Ambrose that exploded on a wet wicket in Trinidad, and before I could do anything it was in third slip's hands. Otherwise, all my dismissals have been avoidable — either bad footwork or judgment or loss of concentration.

David Boon •497

No bugger ever got all ten when I was at the other end.

Sydney Barnes after watching Jim Laker take all ten wickets for England v Australia, Old Trafford, 1956 •498

It has been suggested tonight that no-one may again do what I've been lucky enough to do this season. I don't know about that but I do know this — if he does, he'll be tired.

George Hirst, after scoring over 2,000 runs and taking more than 200 wickets for Yorkshire in a season, 1906 •499

When George Hirst got you out, you were out. When Wilfred got you out, you were out twice, because he knew how to get you out in the second innings too. *Roy Kilner, Yorkshire team-mate, comparing the merits of Wilfred Rhodes and George Hirst* •500

They said to me at The Oval, come
and see our new bowling machine.
Bowling Machine? I said I used
to be the bowling machine.

Alec Bedser in 1989 •501

There's a big difference between being fit and being strong.
Sebastian Coe is fit, but he couldn't bowl all day.
Alec Bedser •502

I always thought that the best
way to contain a batsman was to
get him back into the pavilion.

Alec Bedser •503

If I want to get fit for bowling.
I do a lot of bowling.

Brian Statham, Lancashire and England, 1974 •504

I regard an over as having six bullets in a gun. I use those bullets strategically, to manipulate the batsman into a certain position or state of mind, so that I can eliminate him.
Richard Hadlee •505

It was like batting against the World XI at one end and Ilford Second XI at the other.

Mike Gatting compares Richard Hadlee with the rest of the New Zealand attack •506

Imagine being enclosed in a small illuminated space and being fed a barrage of searching questions by an indefatigable examiner. Your responses are nervous gibberish. It soon became clear that facing Hadlee was a bit like this.
Simon Hughes on Richard Hadlee •507

In the ten years I was at Notts, only a couple of young players ever approached me for advice. I find that amazing and it's an insight into the modern attitude. Maybe some guy has learned a bit from watching me, but as far as talking to me about technique and attitude, forget it. Nobody ever wanted to know. *Richard Hadlee, 1988* •508

My effort should disprove that India cannot produce fast bowlers. For 15 years that has been my one great motivation.

Kapil Dev, passing Richard Hadlee's record of 431 Test wickets •509

There is something reminiscent of a wild animal in the sight of Kapil Dev on the cricket field. He is a restless figure, erect and alert, saucer eyes darting hither and thither, muscles, it seems, twitching like a deer on the lookout for danger.

Christopher Martin-Jenkins, **Cricket Characters** *(1987)* •510

The best death bowler I have ever seen.

Wasim Akram on Ian Austin •511

Eeyore without the joie de vivre.

Mike Selvey on Angus Fraser •512

Essentially good-natured, he had that vital weapon in the fast bowlers armoury, grumpiness. *Simon Hughes on Angus Fraser* •513

Fraser never looks over-lively and once or twice in the West Indies we thought he might not make it back to the end of his run.

Raymond Illingworth defending the absurd omission of Angus Fraser from the 1994/95 Ashes tour •515

A thoughtful raise of the eyebrows and a rueful grin. Or, if it was particularly close, an agonized gurn. *John Westerby,* The Times *on Matthew Hoggard's restraint at the crease* •516

The enigma with no variation.

Vic Marks on Chris Lewis •517

He's a show pony. He's a prima donna. Cork may have talent but he does have an attitude problem. If you think I was bad, my God, he's three times worse.
Geoff Boycott, 1997 •518

I'm clumsy and I can't really be anything else. The only graceful sportsmen as big as me are basketball players. *Derek Pringle, 1991* •519

I think Keith Fletcher is right. England's fast bowlers are as quick as Lillee and Thomson… now.
Greg Chappell responds •521

145

County cricket is not a good competition. They would be facing bowlers who are no more than pie-throwers. They would not learn anything about the game. *Rodney Marsh* •522

England's pace bowlers are making the helmet go out of fashion.

Scyld Berry, the **Observer,** *1981.* •523

It was absolutely crackers. A complete joke. I felt under so much pressure to live up to the comparison.

Phil De Freitas on being one of many new Botham's, 2005 •524

If this England lot were put up against Rutland Thirds they would lose. They would lose heavily. It is the only thing that they are good at.

The Sun *displays its usual rational approach* •525

146

Where the duel between the quick
and the batsman is gladiatorial,
the contest between that batsman
and a spin bowler is more like a
chess match. Anticipation, astuteness
and touch come to the fore in these
subtle exchanges. The spin bowler
is cricket's Machiavelli, taunting
and teasing the opponent with
his knowledge and expertise.

Slow bowling is an art, Mr Kelly, and art is international.

*Arthur Mailey replying to a reprimand from the Australian
manager for giving advice to England leg-break bowler
Ian Peebles on the 1930 Tour, Manchester Test* •526

147

The great thing about spin bowling is that it is an art which can be learnt. In that sense it is different from fast bowling. A fast bowler either has the natural ability to hurl the ball down quickly or he hasn't. And if he can't do it, there is no way you can coach it into him. The reverse is true of spin bowling. I believe you can learn it from scratch. *Ray Illingworth, in* **Spin Bowling,** *1980* •527

…that most precious quality of the first-rate spin bowler: the guts and capacity to stand unshaken under heavy punishment, no matter what blows adverse fortune struck.

C.S. Marriott, **The Complete Leg-Break Bowler** *(1968)* •528

Every young spinner turned into a colourless medium-pacer constitutes a crime against a beautiful game. *David Frith,* **The Slow Men** *(1984)* •529

It's all a matter of inches — those between your ears.
Arthur Milton on spin bowling, 1982 •530

I sometimes feel there are more leg-spinners in cricket fiction than in real cricket nowadays.

John Bright-Holmes, **Lord's and Commons** *(1988)* •531

The mystique surrounding the revolutionary ball was hardly lessened by its being given a name. Indeed, the name of its first regular exploiter (pronounced Bo-san-kay) hinted at something foreign: and therefore not to be trusted!

David Frith on B.J.T. Bosanquet, inventor of the googly •532

You can't smoke 20 a day and bowl fast.

Phil Tufnell •533

Bowlers, in the future as in the past, will be applauded and rewarded far less than batsmen.

Phil Edmonds, **100 Greatest Bowlers** *(1989)* •534

Q: Was there any ball that Hedley Verity bowled that you didn't bowl yourself? **A:**Yes, there was the ball that they cut for four.

Exchange between questioner and Wilfred Rhodes •535

Go on, Hedley, you've got him in two minds. He doesn't know whether to hit you for four or six.

Arthur Wood, Yorkshire wicketkeeper to left-arm spinner Hedley Verity as the South African batsman, H.B. Cameron, took 30 off an over at Bramall Lane in 1935 •536

Cavalier cricket even in wartime seemed to Verity unwarranted and undignified. It was beyond his understanding.

Alan Hill, Hedley Verity *(1986)* •537

I used to bowl tripe, then I wrote it, now I sell it.

Notice above Arthur Mailey's butcher's shop near Sydney. •538

[He] is compounded of tea, leather, patience, and subtlety.

R.C. Roberson-Glasgow on Clarrie Grimmett, **Cricket Prints** *(1943)* •539

For Clarrie Grimmett leg-break and googly bowling was the main reason for living. Taking a cricket ball away from Clarrie during a match was like taking a bone from a dog. *R.S. Whitington,* **Time of the Tiger** *(1970)* •540

To hit him for four would usually arouse a belligerent ferocity which made you sorry. It was almost like disturbing a hive of bees. He seemed to attack from all directions. *Sir Donald Bradman on Bill O'Reilly,* **Farewell to Cricket** *(1950)* •541

Some bowlers and wicket-keepers, and others for that matter, are better at appealing than their mates… Bill O'Reilly, they tell me, was terrifying.

Richie Benaud, **On Reflection** *(1984)* •542

When bowling, he completely dominated the situation. He roared at umpires and scowled at batsman. There was so sign of veneer or camouflage when he appealed, nor were there any apologies or beg pardons when the umpire indicated that the batsman's legs were yards out of line with the stumps.

Arthur Mailey on Bill O'Reilly •543

If Jim Laker is to be credited with one outstanding attribute, it must be that of intelligence: and not merely intelligence, but applied intelligence.

John Arlott, Cricket: The Great Bowlers *(1968)* •544

There is almost a kind of magic in the very name 'Ramadhin'. It seems redolent of mystery and guile.

R.E.S. Wyatt, Three Straight Sticks *(1951)* •545

Bulbous but dreamy eyes, close-cropped hair and loosest of gaits gave Gibbs the appearance of a New Orleans trombonist: but his patience as a spin bowler was immense, his accuracy torture to some. *David Frith on Lance Gibbs,* The Slow Men *(1984)* •546

I'm alright when his arm comes over, but I'm out of form by the time the bloody ball gets here.
Fred Trueman, done in the flight, by Hampshire slow left-armer, Peter Sainsbury •547

When he asked me if I could turn out, I thought he wanted me to play him at golf.

Fred Titmus, after a 'phone call from Don Bennett, Middlesex's secretary, with a recall at the age of 46, 1979 •548

When Bishen Bedi bowled, every day seemed bathed in sunshine.
Pat Murphy, **The Spinner's Turn** *(1982)* •549

A great clockmaker would have been proud to have set Bedi in motion — a mechanism finely balanced, cogs rolling silently and hand sweeping in smooth arcs across the face. *Tony Lewis on Bishen Bedi* •550

The face of a choirboy, the demeanour of a civil servant and the ruthlessness of a rat-catcher.

Geoffrey Boycott on Derek Underwood •551

I must have kept wicket, day in day out, to Derek Underwood for seven years now and I doubt he's bowled ten full-tosses or long-hops in the whole of that time. *Alan Knott, 1972* •552

When you're an off spinner there's not much point glaring at a batsman. If I glared at Viv Richards he'd just hit me even further.

David Acfield, Essex, 1982 •553

I'm glad they hadn't invented Spinvision in my day. It would have shown the ball coming out straight. I'd have been carted. *Vic Marks* •554

He has kept the art of back-of-the-hand spin alive against the odds and one can only pray that he has inspired a generation of imitators.

Christopher Martin-Jenkins on Abdul Qadir, **Cricket Characters** *(1987)* •555

Why go to the nets for two hours when all your mates are down the kebab-house making career-best scores on the Galactic Defender?

Phil Tufnell. Why, indeed? •556

Why is Tufnell the most popular man in the team? Is it the Manuel factor in which the most helpless member of the cast is most affectionately identified with?

Mike Brearley on the public's love-affair with Tuffers •557

All I have to do is bowl loopy-doopies to them and they commit suicide.

Phil Tufnell on West Indian batsmen •558

There was a time when a batsman had more chance of being hit by space debris than being done in the flight by Ashley Giles.
Mike Selvey •559

Talent in the conventional sense can only take you so far. You need nous, a willingness to work hard and an understanding of what you can do for the team. *Ashley Giles on Test cricket* •560

Only his mother would describe him as an athlete.

Derek Pringle on Ashley Giles •561

The game's leading wicket-taker is one of the great masters in Shane Warne, and hard on his heels is a burglar, a thief, a dacoit.
Bishen Bedi doesn't sit on the fence about Murali, 2003 •562

It is just as important for a spin bowler to be
aggressive as it is a fast bowler. We play at a very
high level of arousal, on the edge of fury if you like.

Shane Warne, apologizing for his abuse of Andrew Hudson in Johannesburg •563

I'm not going to tolerate a situation where we
get some hang-up about Warne. We must play
him emphatically, positively, and not develop
a mentality that says 'where are we going to
score runs?' when he comes on to bowl.

Michael Atherton before Warne destroyed England in the Ashes •564

Shane Warne's idea of a balanced diet is a cheeseburger in each hand. *Ian Healy, 1996* •565

My diet is still pizzas, chips, toasted cheese sandwiches and
milkshakes. I have the occasional six-week burst where I
stick to fruit and cereal: it bloody kills me. *Shane Warne* •566

How anyone can spin the ball the width of Gatting boggles the mind.
Martin Johnson on that Shane Warne delivery •567

It it had been a cheese roll, it would never have got past him.
Graham Gooch on that Shane Warne delivery •568

My theory is that he spins the ball too much. When Grimmett or O'Reilly beat your bat, they usually hit the wicket. Warne beats the bat, the wicket and everything. What's the good of that, eh?
R.E.S. Wyatt, former England captain, talking drivel about Warne •569

It's almost beyond my comprehension how someone could take 600 Test wickets. I know how hard I had to work to get 187. *Geoff Lawson marvels at Shane Warne* •572

My wife had an uncle who could never walk down the nave of an abbey without wondering whether it would take spin.

Alec Douglas-Home, former English Prime Minister •573

What would sport be without the cult of personality? Passionless bowlers tilting at windmill batsmen would make for dull viewing indeed. Dennis Lillee tearing his hair out at the antics of a somersaulting and fidgeting Derek Randall is not only great sport, but great drama.

Apparently after one lengthy drinking session after a day's play, he forgot where the team were staying and returned to the ground to sleep under the covers!

Andrew Hignell on FP Ryan, The History of Glamorgan CCC *(1988)* •574

At least if we go down we'll take that bugger Barnes with us.
A C McLaren, during a rough sail back to England •575

However big the crowd or serious the occasion there is something about the cricket of Walter Robins which suggests half-holidays and kicking your hat along the pavement. Perky is the word.
C Robertson-Glasgow, **Cricket Prints** *(1943)* •576

He did really tear his hair, he did really leap off the ground like some figure in a mad Frederick Ashton cricketing ballet.

Dudley Carew on JWA Stephenson, **To The Wicket** *(1946)* •577

You must rinse your hand in the chamber pot every day. The urine hardens them wonderfully.
Herbert Strudwick, former England wicketkeeper •578

There was, perhaps, no more arresting figure on the English cricket scene between the wars, nor one whose personality got across more clearly to the crowd. He was an unashamed showman, believing that people deserved a bit of excitement for their money. *E W Swanton on Percy Fender* •579

He brought a cockney wit and spirit of comedy to the cricket field, counterpoint to the sobriety and refinement of the Lord's atmosphere.
Hon T C F Prittie on Patsy Hendren, Middlesex CCC (1951) •580

A dour remorseless Scot, 130 years after his time. He should have gone to Australia in charge of a convict hulk.
Jack Fingleton on Douglas Jardine •581

Like a music-hall comedian he knew what his audience wanted and saw that they got it.
Rex Pogson on Cec Parkin, Lancashire County Cricket (1952) •582

Duckworth's appeals became a feature of cricket at Old Trafford and all other cricket grounds upon which he appeared. It was not so much an appeal as an assertion.

John Marshall, Old Trafford *(1971)* •583

Bill Alley will go down in cricket history for one unique, unrepeatable feat. Freddie Trueman once had to leave the Somerset dressing room blushing modestly because the lurid language was too much for him.

J.J. Warr, The Cricketer, *1982* •584

Godfrey Evans has said that if people did not think he was showing off, he would have kept without pads.

Alan Knott, Stumper's View *(1972)* •585

He would have been caught at extra cover.

Brian Close's reply to a concerned colleague who, after seeing Closey hit on the head whilst fielding at short leg, asked what would have happened had he been hit on the temple. •586

I would have died for Yorkshire.
I suppose once or twice I nearly did.
Brian Close •587

I always told him that it was a good job he was
left-handed and had his heart on the other side.
Ray Illingworth on Brian Close, 1994 •588

He personifies the best virtues
of Yorkshireness — he doesn't
give a toss for reputation, fights
back when cornered and doesn't
even contemplate defeat.
Michael Parkinson on David Bairstow •589

You don't want to be taking them pills; you
want to get some good Tetley's down you.
David Bairstow recommends his favourite cure-all to a colleague •590

I'm this side of the line, you're that and never the twain
shall meet. If they do I'll break your f∗∗∗ing teeth.
Rodney Marsh to an encroaching spectator •591

This champagne's all right, but the blackcurrant jam tastes of fish.
Derek Randall encounters caviar at a reception on a tour of India •592

He is said to have frequently gone in to bat not knowing his
team's score, dropping his cards to grab his bat and cap.
Jack Pollard on Doug Walters, **Australian Cricket** *(1982)* •593

Fitness training consisted of lengthy games of soccer between the capped and uncapped players. Matches lasted for as long as it took the capped players to win.
Ray East, **A Funny Turn** *(1983)* •594

East, one of the funniest men ever to tread a first-class field, almost certainly did himself a disservice by not leaving his clowning in the dressing room. *David Frith,* The Slow Men *(1984)* •595

His epitaph will be stories he created, stories which became bar room legends around the cricket circuit. Cricketers swap Ray East experiences rather as some people swap Irish jokes.
Graham Gooch, East's Essex colleague, in Out Of The Wilderness, *1985* •596

That load of madmen will never win anything until they learn some self-discipline.
Ray Illingworth shortly before Essex won everything (quoted in Ray East, A Funny Turn, *1983* •597

We used to eat so many salads there was danger of contracting myxomatosis.

Ray East, describing lunchtime offerings on the county circuit, in A Funny Turn, *1983* •598

[He has a] reputation for being awkward and arrogant, probably because he is awkward and arrogant. Works very hard at trying to be controversial and iconoclastic, but basically a pillar of the establishment. *Frances Edmonds on her husband, Phil* •599

Cricket needs its eccentrics, needs such singular men as Edmonds if it is to remain sane. The game will be infinitely poorer if Edmonds is, indeed, the last great amateur.

Simon Barnes, Phil Edmonds: A Singular Man *(1986)* •601

A conversation with him would be 50% shorter if he deleted the expletives.

Mike Selvey on John Emburey •602

The fuckin' fuckers fuckin' fucked.

John Emburey's reply, when asked about the state of his dodgy back. •603

Boon always looked like a smaller, inner layer of a Mervyn Hughes, Russian babushka doll.

All Out Cricket, *2005* •604

You get called a fruitcake because others don't understand what you're doing.
Jack Russell, from his autobiography •605

It's very rewarding being a pain in the arse.

Jack Russell, after a backs-to-the-wall innings in Johannesburg alongside Michael Atherton, 1995 •606

I'm getting dangerously close to ordering a full bottle of wine with my dinner.

Near tee-totaller, Jack Russell, surplus to requirements on tour •607

I'm not going to dance the way they want.

Arjuna Ranatunga in characteristically tough mood in Australia •608

The sort of self flagellating bloke who could have scored every week, but he was so self obsessed that he didn't notice anyone else. Even on the local nudist beach he only admired himself.

Simon Hughes on Dermot Reeve •609

The next thing you know they will be saying I wear stockings and suspenders under my flannels. *Phil Tufnell, after allegations of dope smoking, New Zealand, 1997* •610

He believes himself to be misunderstood by the media and therefore misunderstand by the public at large, and it makes him unhappy. He is not, he insists, the remorselessly dedicated monster he is made out to be. He loves cricket, that's all; that's why he tries so hard. *Barry Norman.* Geoffrey Boycott *(1973) reprinted in* The Observer on Cricket *(1987)* •611

What has been forgotten amid the complicated controversies Boycott has got into, is his ability to play near-perfect against all kinds of bowling and on all kinds of wickets.
Sunil Gavaskar, Idols *(1984)* •612

As I stood at the non-striker's end I felt a wave of admiration for my partner; wiry, slight, dedicated, a lonely man doing a lonely job all these years. What is it that compels Geoffrey Boycott to prove himself again and again among his peers?
Mike Brearley, 1979 •613

We were brought up watching opening batsmen score nine before lunch. If Geoffrey Boycott flashed at a ball outside off stump in the first over of a Test match, questions were asked in Parliament. If he flashed at two, the ravens abandoned the Tower of London.
Brian Viner on the pace of modern Tests •614

I wish I could watch it again and again for ever.

Stuart Wilkinson, on bowling Geoffrey Boycott for 12 during Durham's defeat of Yorkshire in Gillette Cup, 1973 •615

County bowlers are nothing if not philosophical. I'll be there in midsummer, running up to Sir Geoffrey, convincing myself he's going to pad up to a straight one.
Brian Brain on the joys of bowling to Geoffrey Boycott •616

Most cricket critics, who have more power than any other writers in sport, would see Chairman Mao as British Prime Minister before they would give Boycott the vote as England captain. *Ian Wooldridge, Daily Mail •617*

He can be so rude to people that sometimes you just want to punch his lights out.

Mark Nicholas on Geoff Boycott •618

You cannot motivate the team with the word 'I'. Geoff cannot fool anyone; they know he's totally, almost insanely, selfish.

Ian Botham on Geoffrey Boycott •619

Geoff has only two points of view. You are either for him or against him. There is no middle ground.

Brian Close, resigning as Yorkshire chairman •620

He is so dedicated to the perfection of his own batting technique that he is sometimes oblivious to the feelings and aspirations of his team-mates.

Arthur Connell, chairman of the Yorkshire committee, on Boycott, 1978 •621

173

I've been swamped by letters from ordinary Yorkshire members who can't contain their outrage. I've heard from others whose children won't stop crying because they'll never see Geoff bat again at Headingley.

Sid Fielden, head of the pro-Boycott lobby, 1983 •622

Geoffrey Boycott is a very good batsman. I wish I had never met him.

Sid Fielden changes his spots, 1985 •623

My lasting memory will be of the greatest of all counties reduced to a squabbling rabble, a squalid, petty argument, of supporters, once the most loyal and sane of all memberships, torn apart by a cult which regarded one man as greater than the club.

John Hampshire sums up the whole, unseemly affair •624

The only fellow I've met who fell in love with himself at an early age and has remained faithful ever since.

Dennis Lillee on Geoffrey Boycott •625

If Geoffrey had played cricket the way he talked he would have had people queuing up to get into the ground instead of queuing up to leave.

Fred Trueman on Geoffrey Boycott. •626

His ability to be where the fast bowlers aren't has long been a talking point among cricketers.

Tony Greig on Geoffrey Boycott. Greig's claim was utter nonsense •627

The greatest tragedy of his troubled life is that, above all else, in the desire to be admired and loved by everyone, he has this enormous capacity for upsetting people.

Tony Greig on Geoffrey Boycott. A much more accurate appraisal •628

The only thing I'm bloody frightened of is getting out.

Geoffrey Boycott •629

175

I enjoy hitting a batsman more than getting him out. I like to see blood on the pitch. And I've been training on Whisky. *Jeff Thomson, Australian fast bowler* •630

I knocked his helmet straight off his head. It went to pieces and blood came out… I thought it was brains coming out. I think he was pretty happy to be alive. *Thomson on bowling at Martin Crowe* •631

The sound of the ball hitting the batsman's skull was music to my ears.

Jeff Thomson •632

I've always thought the selectors were a bunch of idiots. All they've done now is to confirm it.

Jeff Thomson, omitted from Australian tour party to England, 1981 •633

It was nothing. I bowled a lot quicker than that, but they didn't time us.

Thomson on Shoaib topping 100 mph •634

He couldn't bat to save himself. I bowled to him with a dicky arm during the 1977 tour and he was either dropped four times or made nought.

The ever-likeable Jeff Thomson on Ian Botham •635

I kept smiling at Thomson, hoping to keep him in a good mood.

Ranjit Fernando, 5ft 2in Sri Lankan batsman, as two of his team-mates were hospitalised by Jeff Thomson in a World Cup match, 1975 •636

You can count the number of books I have read on one hand. I don't even think you would fill one hand.

Jeff Thomson, 1975 •638

England's batsman seem to get whipped more often than a saucepan full of spuds these days and when you look at the England attack, it looks like a makeshift outfit that couldn't win an argument with a drovers dog. *Jeff Thomson* •639

I dunno. Maybe it's that 'tally-ho, lads' attitude. You know, there'll always be an England, all that Empire crap they dish out. But I never could cop Poms. *Jeff Thomson* •640

I have on occasions taken a quite reasonable dislike to the Australians. *Ted Dexter, 1972* •641

Cricket has moved forward as a game and become a compelling entertainment for the twenty-first century in spite of, rather than thanks to, those who administrate the game. Over the years the powers that run cricket have proven themselves shallow, witless and spineless with alarming regularity.

It's hard to tell where the MCC ends and the Church of England begins.

J.B. Priestley, 1962 •642

It's no use complaining that cricket is fuddy duddy because I'm afraid it's part of the game.

Doug Insole, former chairman of the TCCB •643

Those who run cricket in this country, especially at the domestic level, are for the most part a self-serving, pusillanimous and self-important bunch of myopic dinosaurs unable to take anything but the shortest-term view of everything.

Henry Blofeld, 2003. My dear old thing, thus has it always been. •644

Especially in matters of discipline, MCC is still portrayed as establishment, reactionary, everlasting public school and Oxbridge, and a power-centre for those who live in London and the home counties.

Tony Lewis, **Double Century** *(1987)* •645

What has to be remembered of course is that he is not an Englishman by birth or upbringing, but only by adoption. It is not the same thing as being English through and through.

John Woodcock on Tony Greig •646

A welfare state cricketer.

E.W. Swanton on the captaincy of M.J.K. Smith •647

I have the greatest affection for the county of my birth, but for the committee as a body, the greatest contempt.

W.G. Grace, resigning as Gloucestershire captain, 1899 •648

Many of your committee members are sitting there for no better reason than it is good for their business or social image to do so. They are status seekers who would as quickly get themselves on the tiddlywinks committee if that game should suddenly acquire prestige.
'Bomber' Wells, Gloucestershire spin bowler, 1970 •649

How many companies of 43 employees have a board of 20?

Bob Evans, Warwickshire Chairman who was sacked in absentia for trying to reduce that number •650

You do have a private income, don't you?
Middlesex committee man to mike Brearley on his appointment as captain •651

The Chairman of the cricket committee would come into the dressing-room just before we were going out to play an important Gillette Cup match and start telling us how Sussex Martlets had got on on Sunday. And he expected us to be interested. *John Snow* •652

For all their dereliction of duty in leaving without permission a game in which they were playing, it was a harsh penalty for an essentially light-hearted prank, reflecting all too accurately the joyless nature of the tour.
Wisden on David Gower and John Morris' airborne prank in Queensland, 1990/91 •654

You've got to get on with the powers that be, to tug the forelock.
Phil Edmonds, 1983 •655

A rebel is a person who disagrees with the committee. *Arthur Mailey* •656

We want Mike to play for England again don't we? What we would like is for you to write two thousand words that are very bland.

Donald Carr, Lord's bigwig, brings less than subtle influence to bear on the content of Mike Gatting's ghost-written autobiography •657

No longer should we allow international cricketers to appear on our television sets to be interviewed unshaven, chewing gum and altogether looking slovenly. These habits are to be deplored and should be eliminated.

Lord MacLaurin, 1998, starting to stir the sheep •658

183

He will see that trying to shake up English cricket is like stirring dead sheep.

Ray Illingworth on Lord MacLaurin's appointment as ECB Chair •659

They bring him out the loft, take the dust sheet off him, give him a pink gin and sit him there. He can't go out of a 30-mile radius of London because he's normally too pissed to get back. He sits there at Lord's, saying that 'That Botham, look at his hair, they tell me he's had some of that cannabis stuff.'
Ian Botham portrays the archetypal selector •660

One criticism levelled at the selectors from many cricket pavilions has been that they are, in general, of an age when active contact with cricket's problems is behind them. *Walter Hammond,* Cricket's Secret History *(1952)* •661

For God's sake don't make a fool of yourself.

Chairman of selectors, Alec Bedser's inspiring words to Alan Butcher before his only Test •662

We were going to sack him anyhow.

Alec Bedser, England's chairman of selectors, on David Gower's resignation •663

185

There is no doubt that Dexter can handle a
bat but who is going to handle Dexter?
England selector after appointment of Dexter as captain, 1962 •664

There is a modern fashion for designer stubble
and some people believe it to be very attractive.
But it is aggravating to others and we shall be
looking at the whole question of people's facial hair.
Ted Dexter gets to the heart of England's problems •665

I think we are all slightly down in the dumps
after another loss. We may be in the wrong sign…
Venus may be in the wrong juxtaposition with
somewhere else. *Ted Dexter, after yet another defeat by Australia, 1993* •666

Who can forget Malcolm Devon?

Ted Dexter shows his familiar grasp of events •667

I'm not aware of any mistakes I've made this summer.
Ted Dexter, after England get caned in the Ashes, 1989 •668

It is possible that some of Dexter's visions might one day become a little more solid. However, he also talked a good deal of tosh in an arrogant tone of voice. For a professional PR man he was extraordinarily unaware of the impression he made. *Matthew Engel* •669

He crossed the line between eccentricity and idiocy far too often for someone who was supposed to be running English cricket.

Ian Botham on Ted Dexter's tenure as Chairman of Selectors •670

The selectors emphasised that they did not believe the allegations in the newspaper and accepted Gatting's account of what happened. The selectors were concerned, however, that Gatting behaved irresponsibly by inviting female company to his room for a drink in the late evening.

The England committee, in typically cowardly vein, allow The Sun's *Test Stars In Sex Orgy headline to cloud their judgment* •671

One is always a little nervous when watching England bat.

Peter May, chairman of selectors, 1994. •672

187

I fear he will be too keen to run the train-set all by himself.

Mike Brearley on Ray Illingworth's appointment as chairman of England selectors •673

One began to feel that the right adjective was the one never attached to him in his playing days: amateurish.

Matthew Engel on Raymond Illingworth as chairman of the England selectors •674

It's not a captain's job to go around criticising selectors.

Raymond Illingworth on Mike Atherton •675

He's not a motivator he's just a whinger.

Allan Lamb on Illingworth's tenure as England manager •676

Illingworth (n) A measure of rich humbug, prob originating in Yorkshire. Used figuratively of person who claims credit for success but blames others for failure. Examples: any interview with the chairman of England's cricket selectors. **Private Eye, 1995** •677

If he could, he would mark man-for-man.

Peter Roebuck on Mickey Stewart •678

I thought suggestions of a father and son business were in the past. For six years as England manager I avoided the words 'dad' and 'son', much to the merriment of the media. The only thing I have ever been concerned about is English cricket.

Mickey Stewart defends the presence of Alec in the England team •679

We're not picking the England team any more on county ability but on character.

Nasser Hussain, Ashes, 2002-03. England still lost but the policy has borne fruit •680

Why are people too old to play Test cricket at 37, but too young to select the team until they are collecting their pension? *Ian Botham* •681

It is rather suitable for umpires to dress as dentists, since one of their tasks is to draw stumps. *John Arlott* •682

If anyone were to ask us the question 'what class of useful men receive most abuse and lest thanks for their service?' We should, without hesitation, reply, 'Cricket umpires'.
A.G. Steel, **The Badminton Library – Cricket** *(1904)* •683

Umpiring is as difficult as batting or bowling.

Learie Constantine, **The Young Cricketer's Companion** *(1964)* •684

I'm in charge of this game, You'll stand where I want you to. If you don't stand there, there won't be a game.
Arjuna Ranatunga gets ideas above his station whilst addressing Umpire Emerson in Australia, 1999 •685

What happened between Gatting and me does not seem so ugly after Broad hitting his stumps. Now Dilley has sworn and everybody in the ground has heard his words. Maybe the cricket public will now agree with me that Gatting has some bad boys in his team.

Shakoor Rana, the umpire at the heart of England's
acrimonious tour to Pakistan in 1987-88 •686

We were never going to be allowed to win by fair means. The team have voted in favour of stopping the tour right now.

Allan Border, Karachi, 1988. The tour continued. •687

I would rather spend eight hours a day undergoing root-canal treatment than function as an international umpire.

Matthew Engel, Wisden *editor, 2005* •688

He arrived on earth from the Planet Looney to become the best and fairest of all umpires. Great bloke, completely bonkers.

Ian Botham on Dickie Bird •689

191

I don't think umpiring can decide the fate of a match.
Mark Taylor refuses to blame partisan umpiring for a defeat in India, 1998 •690

If we have appeared to have batted in a hurry, it is because the batsman want to make the most of their short stay before the umpires do them in.
The Sri Lankans explain away a thrashing by India •691

He was the first umpire to combine the distinct roles of top-flight umpire and music-hall comedian. He was the first umpire superstar. *Matthew Engel, on Dickie Bird* •692

Like politicians, their decisions rarely satisfy both parties.
Vic Marks, TCCB Guide to Better Cricket *(1987)* •693

It's not easy taking up umpiring after being an umpire baiter for over thirty years.
Bill Alley, joining umpires list, 1969 •694

What goes on in the middle is our business, nothing to do with anybody else.

Mervyn Kitchen replying to press questions about no-balling Jeff Thomson, 1985 •695

I learned more in my first year as an umpire than in all the previous twenty-six years of playing the game. *E.J.Smith* •696

You'll never die wondering, son.

Umpire Cec Pepper to Ashley Mallett, a frequent and vociferous appealer •697

Oslear found something in the rules to get off the pitch because of the cold last year, but I can't find the bloody thing. *Dickie Bird, umpiring at Derby* •698

'Time', and that's Sunday lunch, roast beef and all.

David Shepherd, at lunch on Sunday in a Test match. •699

193

Doubt? When I'm umpiring, there's never any doubt!

Frank Chester, legendary Test umpire •700

A lingering death-merchant.

Henry Blofeld on Steve Bucknor, he of the slow finger •701

Hawkeye to me is just a cartoon and I'm yet to work out how that graduate can work out where the ball is going to.

Dick French, former Test umpire, can't do the science •702

It went 29-5 against us — umpires are not cheats, I would never accuse them of that, but I do believe they are influenced by the way teams appeal and by the crowds.

Bob Woolmer doesn't believe Pakistan were beaten fair and square in Australia •703

Derek Underwood could never bowl at my end — he could not get round me.

Swaroop Kishen, heavyweight Indian Test umpire, admission to Dickie Bird (from That's Out, *1985)*•704

Jimmy Burke had an action like a policeman applying a truncheon to a particularly short offender's head. *Ian Peebles* •705

Was I bowled or run out?

Doug Insole, bowled by Tony Locks's quicker ball, **The Rest v Surrey, The Oval (1955)** •706

Bowl him one for a change Burkie, you'll surprise him.

Colleague to Burke, New South Wales pace bowler, during throwing controversy in Australia; MCC tour, 1957/8 •707

195

No umpire enjoys calling bowlers for throwing. It is a very unpleasant task… but someone has to stop illegal bowling.

Tom Smith, General Secretary of the Association of Cricket Umpires, in The Cricketer, July, 1960 •708

If his action is the same as it was, he would be no-balled walking down the gangplank at Tilbury. *England player on Meckiffs illegal action, 1963* •709

It defies description — the feeling that hits players when there is a no-ball called for throwing… The game was carried on by instinct for a while, for the Australian players were not 'with it'.

Richie Benaud, after Meckiff was called for throwing •710

I was filmed so much that I qualified for an Equity card. *Geoff Cope* •711

There are always going to be a lot of whispers and secret letters passed on to people. It's not quite as simple as an umpire putting his arm out.

Mark Taylor, during the Murali row •712

Murali is being tormented because somebody else decided to play God.

Ranjit Fernando, Sri Lankan manager, defends
Murali's action after the Emerson episode •713

Open your fucking eyes!

Aamir Sohail to an umpire in Zimbabwe after seeing Henry
Olonga for the first time. Olonga was duly picked for
Zimbabwe, and duly called for throwing. •714

...The patience of a saint, the diplomacy of an ambassador, the compassion of a social worker and the skin of a rhino.
Ray Illingworth on the attributes required for captaincy •715

Decisiveness has always been an essential quality for captains in a sport which demands much more from its leaders than any other. *Christopher Martin-Jenkins,* Cricket — A Way of Life *(1984)* •716

When I win the toss on a good pitch, I bat. When I win the toss on a doubtful pitch, I think about it a bit and then I bat. When I win the toss on a very bad pitch, I think about it a bit longer, and then I bat. *W.G. Grace* •717

A pessimistic commander. I have heard old timers say he was liable to enter the dressing-room clutching his head and saying 'Look what they've given me this time,' or 'Gracious me! Don't tell me you're playing!' which cannot have been very good for morale.
Ian Peebles on A.C. MacLaren •718

He was a born leader of men and proved one of the outstanding captains in the game's history. His readiness to identify and encourage young cricketers paved the way for several distinguished careers.
Gerald Howart, **Plum Warner** *(1987)* •719

There's only one captain of a side when I'm bowling — me.
Sydney Barnes •720

He was one of the last of the cavalier captains, whose misfortune was to overlap with the roundheads who turned Test cricket into a war of attrition.
Gerry Cotter on A.P.F. Chapman, **The Ashes Captains** *(1989)* •721

A captain cannot make a bad side into a good one, but a great side can make an indifferent captain into a moderate one.
Jardine, **Evening News** *(1933) reprinted in* **An Ashes Anthology** *(1989)* •722

Closer examination of his character and the testimony of those who knew him reveal that posterity has attributed to him sinister qualities which he never in fact possessed.
Christopher Douglas, **Douglas Jardine** *(1984)* •723

I didn't get on with him as a man. We had nothing in common. But as a batsman, captain and tactician, he had no equal.

Keith Miller on Sir Donald Bradman •724

If it was a matter of life and death I would choose to play under Len Hutton. The object of the game was far more important than the game itself. ***Godfrey Evans, The Gloves Are Off, 1961*** •725

May, I should say, is a cavalier batsman and a roundhead captain.

A.A. Thomson, Hirst and Rhodes (1959) •726

One of you bugger off and the rest scatter.

Keith Miller, captaining New South Wales •727

The hallmark of a great captain is the ability to win the toss, at the right time. *Richie Benaud* •728

Captaincy is the ability to think ahead of play, not to be left responding to it. *Richie Benaud* •729

Captaincy is ninety per cent luck and ten per cent skill. But don't try it without that ten per cent.

Richie Benaud •730

Frank Worrell turned West Indies from being the most magnificent group of individual cricketers in the world into a close-knit team. No one else could have done it. *Richie Benaud,* **On Reflection** *(1984)* •731

He could never make up his mind to call heads or tails. *Ray Illingworth on Colin Cowdrey* •732

I would guess that Dexter was more interested in ideas than people. *Mike Brearley* •733

I can tell you what a wicket will do most times by the sound of it, when I tap it with a bat and by the way it looks. *Gary Sobers* •734

Close had the dash, the flair. He would introduce fielding changes which seemed to possess no cricket logic at all and yet produced a wicket.

John Hampshire, **Family Argument** *(1983)* •735

It is doubtful if anyone else had delved so deeply or effectively into the tactics of the various forms of the contemporary game.

John Arlott on Ray Illingworth, **Book of Cricketers** *(1979)* •736

On the field with him you sense that he knows every blade of grass by name. At Lord's, the Father Time weather vane turns by one degree behind his back and he will announce, "wind's on the move."

Tony Lewis on Ray Illingworth •737

It is difficult, though, to believe that Test cricket has ever known a better captain, strategically, above all, in psychological perception and consequent handling of men.

John Arlott on Mike Brearley
The Guardian Book of Sport,
1981/82 •738

All cricket captains bat and field, and some bowl.
We receive repeated intimations of our own fallibility.
J.M. Brearley, **The Art of Captaincy** *(1985)* •739

He must be capable of firm autocratic decisions in a crisis; and of consulting
his team wherever possible. He should intermingle optimism with realism.
J.M. Brearley, **Phoenix from the Ashes** *(1982)* •741

The statistics suggest that he is one of the great England captains. The luckiest would be nearer the truth.
Ray Illingworth with a Yorkshireman's viewof Mike Brearley •743

His clarity of mind enabled him to pierce the woolly romanticism and anachronistic feudalism which for so long obscured the truth of cricket.
John Arlott on Mike Brearley •742

On Friday I watched J.M. Brearley directing his fieldsmen
very carefully. He then looked up at the sun and made a little
gesture which suggested that it should move a little squarer.
Who is this man? *Letter to* **the Guardian** *in 1981* •744

As captain you can never be one of the boys.

Tony Lewis, **Playing Days** *(1985)* •745

You'll have the most miserable time of your life. *Brian Close's advice to Ian Botham on being Captain of England. Prophetic words* •746

Without being unkind, a donkey could head West Indies at the moment. But put Clive Lloyd in charge of Australia and even he'd struggle.

Keith Fletcher, reacting to Kim Hughes' resignation of Australian captaincy, 1984 •747

Captaincy seems to involve half-hearing conversations which you'd rather not hear at all. *Peter Roebuck, Somerset batsman, in* It Never Rains, *1984* •748

You're in charge from the moment you wake up until you buy a pint in the bar for the other players after the game. At times there are so many demands before play starts that I suddenly realise I've had no time for a knock-up myself. *M.C.J. Nicholas on his first season as Captain of Hampshire, 1985* •749

He's tough. Tougher than I thought at first. He is stubborn, but that's no crime — so am I. I think we have more in common than perhaps either of us realised in the beginning.
Ray Illingworth, 1997, of Mike Atherton •750

I'm pretty good at keeping my feet on the ground.
Michael Atherton after a rare England Ashes Test win, at Edgbaston, 1997 •751

My back is my problem. It is not a cause for national concern.

Michael Atherton •752

His captaincy lacked drive, purpose and flair. Add to that his passive body language and you're struggling when the team is up against it. *Dermot Reeve on Michael Atherton* •753

I've watched it all with dismay that people weren't prepared to captain their country. You have to admire their honesty but maybe their mindset is different.
Steve Waugh, after Butcher and Stewart declined to step in for the injured Hussain, 2001 •754

I don't want to think
at the end of my career
that I didn't captain
England simply because
I was misunderstood.

Nasser Hussain after being passed over for the England captaincy by
Alec Stewart. Happily for both England and Nasser, he got his chance •755

What you get from Nasser is
honesty. There aren't many
captains who look you in the
eye and tell you you're a tosser.

Darren Gough •756

The old-fashioned watchers of the game complain about media coverage of cricket; how it intrudes on the game's time-honoured manners and traditions. The truth is, without TV cricket would have died. A game run by and written about by innately conservative and selfish people would have failed to move with the times had it not been dragged kicking and screaming by the broadcasters.

Probably the most celebrated British voice after Churchill's.

Frank Keating on John Arlott •757

My word, I know what the problems are. I've failed at everything.

John Arlott refutes the idea that playing first-class cricket makes a better commentator •758

Exact, enthusiastic, prejudiced, amazingly visual, authoritative and friendly... *Dylan Thomas on John Arlott* •759

Players enjoyed their company. You can't say that about many commentators.

Ian Botham, on the popularity of Brian Johnston and John Arlott •760

His gift was a capacity to invest cricket and cricketers with an heroic status: he interpreted the feelings of the literate cricket enthusiast and, in doing so, changed the entire shape of writing about the game.

John Arlott, **An Eye For Cricket** *(1979)* •761

Cricket is the senior, most widespread, and deeply-rooted of English games.

John Arlott (1968), Reprinted in **The Guardian Book of Cricket** *(1986)* •762

All cricketers are cricketers, none the less so for not being 'first-class', which is no more than a statistical distinction.

John Arlott, **An Eye for Cricket** *(1979)* •763

John Arlott has been that rarity, a man respected by the players as much as the public… somehow Arlott's presence made you feel cricket was in good hands.

Brian Brain. **Another Day, Another Match,** *(1981)* •764

The commentary lost more than just Arlott's unassuming gravitas. When he retired, the commentary team lost much of its humanity.

Simon Barnes, 1991, in a tribute to John Arlott after his death •765

In Arlott's day the radio team had a centre of gravity; in the age of Johnston a centre of levity.

Russell Davies neatly contrasts the two great voices of Test Match Special •766

There is Neil Harvey, with his legs wide open, waiting for a tickle.

A Johnners classic •767

Ray Illingworth has just relieved himself at the pavilion end.

Brian Johnston •768

The batsman's Holding, the bowler's Willey.

Brian Johnston on Test Match Special •769

Welcome to Worcester where we have just seen Barry Richards hit one of Basil D'Oliveira's balls clean out of the ground. *Brian Johnston* •770

The Queen's Park Oval, exactly as the name suggests, absolutely round. *Tony Cozier* •771

On the outfield hundreds of small boys are playing with their balls. *Rex Alston in those innocent early days of radio commentary* •772

Strangely, in slow-motion replays, the ball seemed to hang in the air for even longer. *David Acfield* •773

Gosh, it's difficult to identify these chaps. Sometimes they turn out to be brothers or cousins, and sometimes not to be related at all.

Henry Blofeld on the Pakistani touring side of 1987 •774

Yorkshire 232 all out, Hutton ill — I'm sorry, Hutton 111.

John Snagge reading the sports' news on the BBC •775

I thought they were only allowed two bouncers in one over. *Bill Frindall, BBC Radio 4's Test Match Special scorer on the appearance of a streaker, 1995* •776

Performances in the match will not be included in any records published under my name.

Bill Frindall protests about the ICC ruling that the tsunami relief games were declared official ODIs. Many players have thought themselves bigger than the game, but a scorer? •777

There are good one-day players, there
are good Test players, and vice versa.
[And there's bollocks] Trevor Bailey •778

I think if you've got a safe pair of hands, you've got a safe pair of hands.
Tom Graveney. Included because it was the most exciting thing he ever said on air •779

Test Match Special is all
chocolate cakes and jolly japes,
but I didn't enjoy being called a
wheelie-bin, and nor did my family.

Ashley Giles response to Henry Blofeld's careless remark •780

Test Match Special, like the MCC, Lord's and the
late, ghastly E.W. Swanton, represents the jolly good
chap view of cricket, one that squeals with delight
over a batsman's public school pedigree and still
takes a dim view of wearing shades in the field.
Leo McKinstry, Observer Sport Monthly, *Feb 2005* •781

Judgments by commentators should be made on probability not on outcome. So when Jim Laker writes in *The Express* on Friday that it was a mistake to put Australia into bat at The Oval, one should know that his opinion (given to Paul Parker's father), an hour before the start on Thursday was that we should field. *Mike Brearley* •782

Each word in a bar, each whisper in a lift, each phrase in a press conference, each indiscreet stroke on the pitch, is whacked on the back page, replayed on the TV screens and tut-tutted on the radio. *Mark Nicholas* •783

What do I think of the reverse sweep? It's like Manchester United getting a penalty and Bryan Robson taking it with his head. *David Lloyd, then England coach* •784

So dull is he, tapes of the Willis delivery should be sold in Mothercare as a sleeping aid for fractious toddlers.
The Guardian's *Jim White on Bob Willis' commentary style* •785

I wouldn't enjoy making my living by criticising my former colleagues.

Bob Willis, 1983. Willis went on to make a living criticising his former colleagues •786

Captain Ahab couldn't stop this ship from sinking.

Michael Atherton on the 2004 West Indies •787

There was a slight interruption there for athletics.

Richie Benaud's wry aside on a streaker interrupting play •788

The nearest thing we are ever going to get to the perfect cricket captain. He matched boyish enthusiasm with ceaseless concentration, calculated attack and non-stop encouragement.

Ray Illingworth on Richie Benaud, **Captaincy** *(1980)* •789

Benaud has always had the will to challenge the bowler. In fact, he has, both as batsman and captain, waged unceasing war against stodge. *A.G. Moyes,* **Benaud** *(1962)* •790

Batting is a major trial before an 11-man jury. *Richie Benaud* •791

They took me down to Newbury for the autumn meeting to trail round after Peter O'Sullivan and it was the best training I could possibly have. He was the most organised man I've ever seen on television.

Richie Benaud •792

In many ways Richie has been the Hemingway of the airwaves, treating us to an economy of words and style… Often, he leaves things partially unsaid, which is inclusive for the viewers as it makes them work just that little bit harder.

Mike Atherton on Richie Benaud, 2005 •793

The Bradman of the commentary box.

Mark Nicholas on Richie Benaud, 2005 •794

The golden age is always well behind us; we catch sight of it with young eyes, when we see what we want to see. *Sir Neville Cardus, Cricket (1930)* •795

We want to admire the stars for what they are as well as for what they do; which is why the exhibitionist antics of a few in recent times, giving the worst of examples to the young watchers on television, are so particularly abhorrent.
E.W. Swanton •796

I have thumbed through the MCC coaching manual and found that no such stroke exists.

Peter May after Ian Botham played a reverse sweep •797

If we had shown the kind of attitude and guts during the war that our cricketers have in the West Indies, Hitler would have walked all over us. *Brian Close, 1986* •798

McCartney or Woolley would have killed Laker. And without referring to my Wisden I could name twenty more batsmen who would have driven the good-looking off-breaker into the dust. *Arthur Mailey on Laker's 19 wickets for 90 runs v Australia, Old Trafford, 1956* •799

When I see a young man who has an expensive and pretty hair-do, I have doubts as to his ability to reach Test standard. *Ted Dexter* •800

England won't improve in world terms until the younger players rediscover some professional pride. *Bob Taylor* •802

These experts are spoiling the market for the others. They are no journalists — the mere writing of articles does not make one a journalist. You have to go through the mill, then develop specialisation. Anyway, no cricketer I have ever known was able to write well. *Alex Bannister,* Daily Mail *correspondent* •803

We didn't have metaphors in my day. We didn't beat about the bush.

Fred Trueman •804

I'd throw them off the top of the pavilion.
Mind, I'm a fair man. I'd give them a 50-50 chance.
I'd have Keith Fletcher underneath trying to catch them.
Fred Trueman, on the saboteurs of the Test wicket, 1975 •805

I'd have looked even faster in colour.

Fred Trueman •806

There's only one head bigger than Greig's, and that's Birkenhead.

Fred Trueman. Surely you've forgotten one other, Fred... •807

Tell me, Fred, have you ever bowled a ball which merely went straight?

Richard Hutton's lugubrious enquiry to Fred Trueman during their Yorkshire playing days •808

Fast bowlers wearing earrings? I don't know what the game's coming to.

Fred Trueman, 1982. The bowler was Derek Pringle •809

He couldn't bowl a hoop downhill.

Fred Trueman on Botham •810

I've just spent a month working on training videos for the English Cricket Board. I'm pretty sure that they wouldn't have used me if they were worried about my action.

Darren Gough, after Fred Trueman expressed doubts about his action in 1997. •811

It's a bloody disgrace. Anybody not born in this great county — no matter who he is — shouldn't be allowed to take the field for Yorkshire. When I was playing we beat everybody in sight and there's no reason why we can't do it again. All we have to do is get rid of half the committee and replace them with people who actually know something about cricket. *Fred Trueman* •812

Let this lot [Yorkshire, 2001] win six or seven championships, then I'll compare 'em seriously with the side of the 60s.

Trueman. Who else? •813

They're not bad this lot, but if we played 'em on uncovered wickets we'd give 'em an innings start.

Illingworth, that's who •814

In among the more familiar sound of this summer —
Richie Benaud's 'Morning everyone' and Adam Gilchrist's
growled 'Good area, Shane' — one familiar note has been missing.
We have not heard commentators saying it was much better in their day;
we have, for once, rid ourselves of curmudgeons and cynics.

Tim Adams in The Observer •815

There is nothing I have detested more than the way in which elder men have said that their young days had the best. Cricket is constantly in flux.

Sir Home Gordon, Background of Cricket *(1939)* •816

The golden age is behind us. But then it always was.

Benny Green •817

Cricket is the easiest sport in the world to take over.
Nobody bothered to pay the players what they were worth.
Kerry Packer, 1977 •818

It makes me laugh when I hear the anti-Packer lobby telling me how to spend my winters. When I was a teenager, the same sort of people did not give a damn what I did between September and April. *Gordon Greenidge, 1980* •819

The Administrators have had 100 years
to improve pay and conditions for the
players and they haven't made any progress.
Mushtaq Mohammed on the breakaway Packer circus, 1977 •820

An example of the Lord's guidance came for me with my decision to join Packer's World Series Cricket. *Alan Knott,* It's Knott Cricket, *1985* •821

His action has inevitably impaired the trust which existed between the cricket authorities and the captain of the England side.

TCCB cricket council, sacking Tong Greig as England's captain after announcement of Packer Circus, 1977 •822

You British reckon everything can be solved by compromise and diplomacy. We Australians fight to the very last ditch.

Kerry Packer, 1978 •823

There is a little bit of the whore in all of us, gentlemen, don't you think?

Kerry Packer, meeting Australian Board of Control to discuss TV rights, 1976 •824

The sportsman has ceased to be a hero. To achieve heroic status, the hero must put something ahead of his own personal interests.

Michael Davie, **The Packer Revolution** *(1977) reprinted in* **The Observer on Cricket** *(1987)* •825

Why should I buy cricket? Nobody watches it.

Greg Dyke, then Head of ITV sport, 1988 •826

If I had my time again, I would never have played cricket.
Why? Because of people like you. The press do nothing but
criticise. *Gary Sobers* •827

> They smile and then they stab — and
> they think the next time they come
> along for a comment you are going to
> forget the wounding things they write
> and obligingly talk to them.
>
> *Geoffrey Boycott on the Press* •828

By 2000 the TV cameras will be everywhere: dressing room,
hotel and bathroom. I visualize the newsman's mania for
live human action and reaction breaking all bounds of privacy
and decency. *Tony Lewis, 1969. Blimey, he had a good crystal ball* •829

227

Newspapers are only good enough for wrapping up fish and chips. They are the pits. *Martin Crowe* •830

If anybody had told me I was one day destined to make a reputation as a writer on cricket I should have felt hurt. *Neville Cardus,* **Autobiography,** *1947* •831

The taste of blood stimulated the Australians; they are terrible when they feel a grip on their prey, almost carnivorous. *Neville Cardus* •832

Halfway between the 10 Commandments and Enid Blyton.

J.J. Warr on E.W. Swanton •833

I knew I could never be a 'real' newspaper journalist — it was such a difficult job to be hail-fellow-well-met-what's-yours-old-boy in private life and next day have to scalpel-slash a reputation in public print.

Frank Keating, **Another Bloody Day in Paradise,** *1981* •834

It couldn't have been Gatt. Anything he takes up to his room after nine o'clock he eats.

Ian Botham explains why allegations of Mike Gatting cavorting with a barmaid must be false •836

Ted Dexter is to journalism what Danny La Rue is to Rugby League.

Michael Parkinson. •837

I will never be accepted by the snob press.

Working-class hero, Ray Illingworth •838

You don't get people going round saying "Did it work for you?" and "It seems to me there's a sense in which…" like those awful scum on late-night BBC2 shows.

Stephen Fry in 1999 on why he enjoys the conversation watching cricket •839

More than any other game, even golf and baseball, cricket has been documented by literary talents. The obsessive nature of the game inspires its followers to put themselves on paper in its praise (or otherwise). The result? Some patchy poetry and far from purple prose... dear reader, turn the page at your peril!

To want something so badly that it hurts can be endured. To need something as much as breath itself can be dangerous. Ramprakash was troubled because he was obsessed.

Peter Roebuck gets all Shakespearean over the failure of Mark Ramprakash at test level •840

In their youth they feared they might never be able to test themselves in the highest company. Has not the poet written that 'full many a flower is born to blush unseen and waste its sweetness on the desert air'?
Peter Roebuck gets all flowery about Zimbabwe's Flower brothers •841

His game embraced a contempt for his fate, a foaming fury, because to him, cricket was a game of kill or be killed, a street fight in which it was left to the umpires to keep peace.
Peter Roebuck on Viv Richards •842

His innings had all the familiar traits: defiance, a terrible stillness at execution, chiselled defence… Waugh's innings was slipped, capable, discriminating and withering. Every ball passed through the laboratory of his mind and no stroke was played without the most careful consideration.
Peter Roebuck on Steve Waugh in 1997 •843

His googly remains as hard to read as James Joyce and his deliveries turned and bounced sharply from a dusty surface.
Peter Roebuck on Stuart MacGill •844

He needs to leave the game and might not, for it is a tribe and he counts himself among its chiefs.

Peter Roebuck on Mike Atherton, who has made a decent career in the media despite Roebuck's advice •845

His instincts are not tamed, his zest for life has not mellowed. His whole-heartedness leads to triumphs and troubles, to success and scrapes, for it is not balanced by a shrewd appreciation of public relations nor by a tolerance of rudeness or criticism. *Peter Roebuck on Ian Botham,* **Slices of Cricket** *(1982)* •846

He never exploited the game, he needed the game. He was a character who made the game grow and who grew himself because of the game. *Peter Roebuck on Dickie Bird* •847

His air of enigmatic simplicity is as cultivated as his garden. It is designed to create an impression of mystical wisdom.

Peter Roebuck on Keith Fletcher, **Men of Essex** *(1984)* •848

Cricket more than any other game is inclined
towards sentimentalism and cant.

*Neville Cardus, who more than any other cricket
writer was inclined towards...* •849

Cricket. A sport in which contenders drive a ball with sticks in opposition to each other.

Dr Johnson, Dictionary of the English Language, *1755* •850

Together we impell'd the
flying ball: Together waited
in our tutor's hall: Together
joined in cricket's manly toil.

Lord Byron, Cricket at Harrow in Hours of Idleness
(1807) •851

Who would think that a little bit of leather, and two pieces of
wood, had such a delightful and delighting power!

Mary Russell Mitford, Our Village *(1824-32)* •852

234

Oh, I am so glad you have begun to take an interest
in cricket. It is simply a social necessity in England.
P.G. Wodehouse, Piccadilly Jim *(1917)* •860

I see them in foul dug-outs, gnawed by rats,
And in the ruined trenches, lashed by rain,
Dreaming of things they did with balls and bats.

Siegfried Sassoon, The Dreamers *(1917)* •861

I bowl so slow that if after I have delivered the ball I don't
like the look of it, I can run after and bring it back. *J.M. Barrie* •862

It is said, I believe, that to
behold the Englishman at
his best one should watch
him play tip-and-run.

Ronald Firbank, The Flower Beneath The Foot, *1923* •863

Now in Maytime to the wicket,
Out I March with bat and pad;
See the son of grief at cricket,
trying to be glad. *A.E. Housman:* A Shropshire Lad, *1896* •854

A Bat, a Ball, two wickets and a Field —
What words are these that can such magic yield?
George Francis Wilson, **A Century of Fours, from Cricket Poems** *(1905)* •856

'The last time I played in a village cricket match,'
said Psmith, 'I was caught at point by a man in
braces. It would have been madness to risk another
such shock to the system.' *P.G. Wodehouse,* **Mike,** *1909* •857

His lightest interest was cricket, but he did not take that lightly.
His chief holiday was to go to a cricket match, which he did as
if he was going to church: and he watched critically, applauded
sparingly, and was darkly offended by any unorthodox play.
H.G. Wells, **The History of Mr Polly** *(1910)* •858

I wish you'd speak to Mary, Nurse,
She's really getting worse and worse.
Just now when Tommy gave her out
She cried and then began to pout
And then she tried to take the ball
Although she cannot bowl at all.
And now she's standing on the pitch,
The miserable little bitch!
Hilaire Belloc, **The Game of Cricket** •859

Drinking the best tea in the world on an empty cricket ground — that, I think, is the final pleasure left to man.

C.P. Snow,
Death Under Sail,
1932 •868

The sun in the heavens was beaming;
The breeze bore an odour of hay,
My flannels were spotless and gleaming,
My heart was unclouded and gay;
The ladies, all gaily apparelled,
Sit round looking on at the match,
In the tree-tops the dicky-birds carolled,
All was peace til I bungled that catch

P.G. Wodehouse, **Missed!** *(first Stanza)* •869

Some boys of course did not enjoy cricket, and we wondered at them, and thought them unsocial.

Edmund Blunden, **Cricket Country** *(1944)* •870

Cricket, lovely cricket, at Lord's where I saw it;
They gave the crowd plenty fun;
Second Test and West Indies won,
With these two little pals of mine,
Ramadhin and Valentine.

Lord Beginner, **Victory Calypso,** *1950* •871

Oh, goodness, what a clinking game cricket was! Splendid even to watch.

Hugh de Selincourt, **The Cricket Match** *(1924)* •864

I played cricket the first season, but resigned because the team seldom consisted of the best eleven men available; regular players would be dropped to make room for visiting gentry.

Robert Graves, **Goodbye to All That** *(1929)* •865

Spedegue had got his fifty-foot trajectory to a nicety, bowling over the wicket with a marked curve from the leg. Every ball fell on or near the top of the stumps. He was as accurate as a human howitzer pitching shells.

Arthur Conan Doyle, 1929, **The Story of Spedegue's Dropper** •866

Casting a ball at three straight sticks and defending the same with a fourth.

Rudyard Kipling, quoted by Sir Neville Cardus in **Cricket** *(1930)* •867

Spooner: How beautiful she was, how tender and how true. Tell me with what speed she swung in the air, with what velocity she came off the wicket, whether she was responsive to finger spin, whether you could bowl a shooter with her, or an off-break with a leg-break action. In other words, did she google?

Harold Pinter, No Man's Land *(1975)* •876

You can have sex either before cricket or after cricket — the fundamental fact is that cricket must be there at the centre of things. *Harold Pinter, 1980* •877

Cricket is full of glorious chances and the Goddess who presides over it loves to bring down the most skillful player.

Thomas Hughes, from Tom Brown's Schooldays •853

I tend to believe that cricket is the greatest thing that God ever created on earth.

Harold Pinter, Pinter on Pinter *in* The Observer *(1980)* •878

239

It is good to bowl with action high or to smite the leather hard and far,
But it's better to wear the proper tie and to keep your end up at the bar

Donald Hughes, **The Short Cut** *(1957)* •872

But after all it's not the winning that matters, is it? Or is it?
It's — to coin a word — the amenities that count; the smell of
the dandelions, the puff of the pipe, the click of the bat, the
rain on the neck, the chill down the spine, the slow exquisite
coming on of sunset and dinner and rheumatism.

Alistair Cooke •873

Half the joy of cricket is playing the innings over again in your mind afterwards.

Christopher Hollis •874

Moon: Sometimes I dream of revolution, a
bloody coup d'etat by the second rank — troupes
of actors slaughtered by their understudies,
magicians sawn in half by indefatigably smiling
glamour girls, cricket teams wiped out by
marauding bands of twelfth men.

Tom Stoppard, **The Real Inspector Hound,** *1968* •875

Miriam: I don't know if I prefer Rog to have a good innings or a bad one: If it's a good one, he relives it in bed, shot by shot, and if it's a bad one he actually replays the shots until he gets it right. He can make a really good innings last all winter

From Richard Harris's play Outside Edge •879

There is nothing wrong with the game that the introduction of golf carts wouldn't fix… It is the only competitive activity of any type, except perhaps baking, in which you can dress in white from head to toe and be as clean at the end of the day as you were at the beginning. *Bill Bryson,* **Down Under** *(2000)* •880

The underprivileged people of America play some strange game with a bat that looks like an overgrown rolling pin. *Fred Trueman,* **English Cricketer** •881

Cricket is basically baseball on Valium.

Robin Williams •882

I want to play cricket, it doesn't seem to matter whether you win or lose.

Meatloaf, US rock singer, 1984 •883

Personally, I have always looked upon cricket as organised loafing.

William Chesterfield in a letter to his son then at Eton, 1740s •890

Cricket needs brightening up a bit. My solution is to let the players drink at the beginning of the game, not after. It always works in our picnic matches.

Paul Hogan, Australian comedian, 1983 •891

I thought it was a bit rude when the umpire gestured to me with a finger so I showed my middle one back.

Eccentric Finnish footballer Aki Rihilati doesn't quite cotton on •892

The three stumps are the triple fold muse of three fates — which must be in balance. The two bails as a man and woman, are balanced on their fates to make up the fivefold wicket which must be defended against the fiery red sun.

Tim Sebastian, Arch Druid of Wiltshire, presents a petition for the return of Stonehenge Cricket Club's ground •902

How can you tell your wife you are just popping out to play a match and then not come back for five days?

Rafa Benitez, Liverpool FC manager, shows why cricket never took off in Spain •894

243

I'd like to thank Denis Compton, a boyhood hero of mine.
Sir Tim Rice, collecting an Oscar, and confusing America in the process •884

Sometimes people think it's like polo, played on horseback, and I remember one guy thought it was a game involving insects. *Clayton Lambert on cricket in the USA* •885

Of all the races in the Galaxy, only the English could possibly revive the memory of the most horrific wars ever to sunder the Universe and transform it into into what I'm afraid is generally regarded as an incomprehensibly dull and pointless game.
Douglas Adams, Life, The Universe and Everything •899

Members and Friends. That's the most ambiguous notice I've ever seen.
Groucho Marx at Lord's in the 1960s •887

A cricketer — a creature very nearly a stupid as a dog.
Bernard Levin, 1965 •888

It requires one to assume such indecent postures.

Oscar Wilde explains his aversion to cricket •889

If Warne is a once-in-a-lifetime bowler, and it is impossible to separate McGrath and Warne, then McGrath must also be a once-in-a-lifetime bowler. Furthermore, Gillespie is as good a quick as has been seen so therefore must be as good as McGrath and hence also a once-in-a-lifetime bowler. If Warne's once-in-a-lifetime tag is a result of what he has done for spin bowling, then since Lee will do the same for fast bowling as Warne did for spin, he must also deserve the once-in-a-lifetime tag. Therefore, Warne, McGrath, Gillespie and Lee are all once-in-a-lifetime bowlers, added to MacGill, a once-in-a-generation bowler. No wonder the Australian test team is so formidable.

A tongue in cheek assessment of Steve Waugh's praise for his team, from a Website blog •903

245

I don't think I can be expected to take that seriously a game which takes less than three days to reach its conclusion.

Tom Stoppard, playwright and cricket buff, on baseball in New York, 1984 •895

There is, of course, a world of difference between cricket and the movie business… I suppose doing a love scene with Racquel Welch roughly corresponds to scoring a century before lunch. *Oliver Reed* •896

The gesture demonstrates the sublimated socially acceptable face of the homo-erotic impulse that makes sport possible.

Oliver James, a psychiatrist, studies a photograph of two Test cricketers celebrating a wicket and comes to a completely crap conclusion •901

I have often thought what a pity it is — how much better a life I would have had, what a better man I would have been, how much healthier an existence I would have led, if I had been a cricketer instead of an actor. But it was not to be.

Lord Olivier, My Life in Cricket (The Twelfth Man, 1971) •898

The hi-jacking of sport for political or commercial capital is no new phenomenon. Such a vital part of the social infrastructure will never be left alone by the power-mongers. This influence and wealth never comes uncluttered by corruption and impropriety — such is life, such is sport, such is cricket.

Say that cricket has nothing to do with politics and you say that cricket has nothing to do with life.

John Arlott •904

247

Bolshevism is rampant, and seeks to abolish all laws and rules, and this year cricket has not escaped its attack. *Lord Harris, 1922, apparently upset because Wally Hammond chose to play for Gloucestershire rather than Kent* •905

Sport is politicised the moment nation-states take the decision to enter the sporting arena under their national banners. England, Australia, India, Pakistan — these are nation-states, not sporting clubs. *Asif Iqbal* •906

If the French noblesse had been capable of playing cricket with their peasants, their chateaux would never have been burned.

G M Trevelyan, **English Social History** *(1944)* •907

This picturesque view is, to my mind, open to question. It is surely more probable that the combination of Latin temperament and bodyline bowling would have accelerated it (the Revolution). *Ian Peebles* •908

Sporting boycotts have become
the shop-soiled currency of
international diplomacy…
some sportsmen are not very
adept at political complexities.

The Guardian *editorial, 1982* •909

He brings to the fierce struggle
of politics the tepid enthusiasm
of a lazy summer afternoon at
a cricket match. *Aneurin Bevan,
on Clement Attlee* •910

It's rather like sending in your opening
batsman only for them to find that their
bats have been broken by the team captain.
*Sir Geoffrey Howe resigns from Thatcher's cabinet with
a neat analogy* •912

There will be no stone-walling, no ducking
the bouncers, no playing for time. The bowling's
going to get hit all around the ground.
*Thatcher responds defiantly, but was still ousted
as Tory leader later* •913

Cricket civilises people and creates good gentlemen. I want everyone to play cricket in Zimbabwe; I want us to be a nation of gentlemen.

Robert Mugabe 1984 •914

A player hesitates over a decision on TV and gets fined, or has a bat logo too large and gets the same treatment. A whole nation's cricket fraternity is about to collapse, and because of some weird rule in the constitution, it cannot get involved.

Henry Olonga on the ICC •915

We are mourning the death of democracy in our beloved Zimbabwe. We cannot in good conscience take to the field and ignore the fact that millions of our compatriots are starving, unemployed and oppressed.

Andy Flower and Henry Olonga, 2003 •916

There are no problems in Zimbabwe. Security is fine.
Heath Streak before the 2003 World Cup, days after Mugabe's government imprisoned his father •917

There are people who put their own dismal prejudices, their half-baked colonial chippiness and their enjoyment of the agreeable futilities of sport ahead of these terrible things. They would prefer to whinge on about the arrogance of the English than consider the genuine evil of Mugabe. They… are wallowing in wilful ignorance.
Simon Barnes on the Zimbabwe Affair, 2004 •918

What a weak and cynical body of men are the decision-makers of the International Cricket Council… they display all the moral integrity of your average bailiff. The Observer's *Kevin Mitchell on same, 2004* •919

Few of those within the world of first-class cricket are political animals. That, however, is no excuse for being politically unconscious.

John Arlott on the Basil D'Oliveira affair, 1968 •920

A particular generation of cricketers thinks in a certain way and only a change in society, not legislation, will change the prevailing style. *CLR James* •921

He revolted against the revolting contrast between his first-class status as a cricketer and his third-class status as a man.

CLR James on Learie Constantine •922

As soon as I got into the West Indies team in the early Seventies it was clear to me that the Asian guys were not going to get fair treatment. It has always been there, but it has just grown and grown. *Alvin Kallicharran* •923

When you are black you never really know what is inside another man's heart.

Viv Richards •924

I buy my newspapers from them.

Trevor Bailey provides conclusive evidence that he harbours no prejudice against Pakistanis •925

Because they are white, I am sorry to say, and I am black, I am out of cricket and they're still playing.

Salim Malik on the difference between his ban and the treatment of Shane Warne and Mark Waugh •926

There can be no normal sport in an abnormal society.

Stance of South African Cricket Board, who run non-white competitions •927

Teams comprising whites and non-whites from abroad cannot be allowed to enter.

Jan De Clerk, South Africa's Minister of the Interior, in a written directive to sports organisation before the Basil D'Oliveria affair •928

Guests who have ulterior motives usually find they are not invited.

PM Vorster, of South Africa, makes their position clear on D'Oliveira •929

I wanted to be a cricketer who had been chosen as a cricketer and not as a symbol.

Basil D'Oliveira •930

It's not the MCC team. It's the team of the anti-apartheid movement. We are not prepared to have a team thrust upon us.

South Africa's Prime Minister Vorster when Basil D'Oliveira was drafted into the MCC tour party in place of the injured Tom Cartwright, 1968 •931

His behaviour in what might have been difficult situations has always been impeccably dignified and courteous.

John Arlott on Basil D'Oliveira, 1968 •932

This is a matter of principle. I like to judge people for what they are, not for what they look like.

Peter Lever, asking to be released from Lancashire contract, for anticipated South Africa visit to Old Trafford, 1970 •933

255

My greatest wish is to see South Africa back in Test cricket.

Fred Trueman, 1979 •934

As far as I was concerned, there were a few people singing and dancing and that was it.

Mike Gatting, captain of the rebel cricketers, turns a blind eye to the dogs, tear gas and baton charges by the police •935

What happens in the townships is nothing to do with us.

Gatting again, in full-on Pontius Pilate mode •936

How can you play cricket with a bloke and then not be allowed to sit in a railway carriage with him?

Ken McEwan, after Colin Croft is thrown off a 'whites-only' section of a South African train, 1983 •937

Dirty money earned by the dirty dozen.

The then Labour Party Leader Neil Kinnock on the rebel tour to South Africa, 1982 •938

When I toured South Africa with Oxbridge Jazzhats, I became physically ill for a week. We were being used for propaganda. I will never return there. *Derek Pringle, 1982* •939

About now your foreign secretary, Douglas Hurd, is in an Alexandria township with the boys of our development programme. Their progress must remain the most important thing. On this of all days, we must keep our priorities.

Dr Ali Bacher, who led South Africa out of cricket's wilderness •940

Pitches are like wives — you can never tell how they're going to turn out.

Len Hutton explains why he fielded after winning the toss. Or not. •941

There are men who fear women more than they love cricket.

DLA Jephson, on club tours •942

Let them in and the next thing you know the place will be full of children.

Lancashire member opposes the resolution to allow women in the Old Trafford, 1985 •943

The MCC should change their name to MCP.

Diana Edulji, Indian women's captain, after being refused entry to the Lord's pavilion during the men's Test, 1986 •944

You can't come in here — you are a lady.

Brisbane gateman to Frances Edmonds (who was in possession of an access all areas Press Pass). See it's not just the English •945

Ladies playing cricket — absurd. Just like a man trying to knit.

Len Hutton •946

Girls! It's absolutely outrageous.

Robin Marlar, 2005. Good to see there's a moderniser in situ at the head of the MCC •947

Absurd, old-fashioned and patronising.

Clare Connor, captain of England's women, is restrained in her response •948

We've always set the trend. Remember, women cricketers were the first to bowl overarm. *Rachel Heyhoe-Flint* •949

Controversy has always been part of cricket.
It titillates and enlivens the human fabric.
Much of it is unseemly but we are inclined
to relish it in retrospect. *David Foot,* Cricket's
Unholy Trinity *(1985)* •950

Use every weapon within the rules, and
stretch the rules to breaking point, say I.
Fred Trueman, 1961 •951

It was the most beautiful-smelling ball I'd ever come across.
*Harold Gimblett's wry observation on a ball shone
with Alf Gover's hair oil, 1930's* •952

It was an act of cowardice and I consider it appropriate that the Australian team were wearing yellow.

*Robert Muldoon, NZ PM, on Greg Chappell's instruction to brother, Trevor, to bowl an
underarm delivery in a ODI against NZ, with six needed to win off the final ball, 1981* •953

When Randall was run out backing up I thought
that if it had been my school the bowler would
have been beaten for it by the housemaster — and
quite right too. *Phil Edmonds on New Zealand v England,
1977/78* •954

We can only guess at Allan Lamb's motives for this article in the Daily Mirror, but we hope that they are nothing to do with money, or even worse, our nationality.
Wasim Akram and Waqar Younis, as England batsman Allan Lamb led a belligerent campaign against alleged ball-tampering, 1992 •955

We have to be whiter than white. I wouldn't really think Michael has done anything illegal but I didn't want him to have this round his neck for the rest of his life.
Raymond Illingworth on the dirty pockets affair, excusing what some saw as a betrayal of Mike Atherton •956

It will go down as one of the most absurd pronouncements of all time because he used dirt. He used dirt to dry his finger. They are doing that every day of the week except that he chose to save time, for which he ought to be applauded. *David Frith, Atherton's staunchest advocate* •957

Following several days of anger, bewilderment and sadness at the furore following the dirt-in pocket incident, I have been struck by its similarity to that of the woman taken in adultery (John ch, viii)... in both cases the accusers are guilty of hypocrisy. The scribes and pharisees of Jesus' time are now represented by the media hacks and self-styled experts of today.
Rev Andrew Wingfield-Digby, former England chaplain, sees holes in the prosecution of Atherton •958

Virtually all bowlers would have to say that they have tampered with the ball at some stage during their county career. *Angus Fraser* •960

The image and integrity of what was once a game, but is now a business is damaged in the eyes of all.

Justice Cooke, the judge who jailed three Pakistani cricketers, summing up after their trial for spot-fixing •961

I got a terrible surprise when he kicked me. I lifted
my bat to ward him off and to tell him if he hit me,
I would hit him... he kept saying dirty words to me.

*Javed Miandad, Pakistan batsman, kicked by Australian pace bowler Dennis
Lillee, Perth, 1981* •962

Javed Miandad is no angel. He's an irritating
little character who keeps baiting people.

Tony Greig on the incident with Dennis Lillee kicking Javed Miandad •963

You don't get good players out by sledging.

Imran Khan •964

I can't think of any player who has
been put off his game by verbal abuse.

*Mark Taylor, who introduced a measure of restraint to the Aussies
on-field behaviour* •965

You never intimidate a good player.

Greg Chappell, in Howzat, *1980* •966

263

When you come back from Australia, you feel you've been in Vietnam. *Glenn Turner* •967

It's just like a zoo out here!
Tim Curtis on playing Dermot Reeve's Warwickshire side, 1995 •968

A six-foot blond-haired beach bum bowling at 90mph trying to knock your head off and then telling you you're a feeble-minded tosser... where's the problem?

Michael Atherton revels in the Ashes atmosphere, 2001 •969

He must enjoy playing cricket... by the end of most games he can't have any match fee left. There's aggression and aggression, but when it happens every ball it just gets boring.

Ian Botham on Andre Nel •970

264

They are the greatest bunch of sledgers there have ever been. These boys get into a bit of trouble and it all comes out. Every bit of badness in them. All I can say is I'm disgusted.
Former Test batsman Neil Harvey on Steve Waugh's side •971

I can hear you my Lord, but where are you?

John Newman (Hampshire) joining his captain, Lionel Tennyson, at the wicket in bad light •972

Too high? If the ball had hit his head it would have hit the bloody wickets!

Alan Brown of Kent, denied an lbw appeal against Lancashire batsman, Harry Pilling (5 ft 3in), 1960's •973

Let's cut out some of the quick singles. OK, Ken, we'll cut out yours.

Exchange between Ken Barrington and Fred Titmus towards end of a hot day in Australia •974

Gower: Do you want Gatt a foot wider?
Cowdrey (the bowler): No, he'd burst.

A legendary on-field exchange •975

265

Don't get him out just yet, Johnny, he smells so bloody lovely.
Yorkshire 'keeper Don Brenan begs Johnny Wardle to leave an
edgy undergraduate at the crease in The Parks •976

I would just like to say that it's a privilege to be sharing the same sporting arena with someone who is bigger than the game. *Angus Fraser has a go at Brian Lara at The Oval, 1995* •977

What number is Snow White batting?
John Emburey to Mike Gatting, playing for Middlesex against Glamorgan;
Batsmen Cottey, Dalton and Phelps were none of them over 5'6" •978

Bad luck, Sir — you were just getting settled in.
Yorkshire's Fred Trueman to a University batsman, clean bowled first
ball after lengthy limbering-up and gardening at the wicket •979

Don't swat those flies Jardine — they're the only friends you've got in Australia.
Adelaide barracker Bodyline series, 1932/3 •980

C'mon Davo, lead him into temptation!

Voice on Sunday Hill, Alan Davidson bowling to Rev. David Sheppard.
MCC tour of Australia, 1963 •981

It beats Monday morning at Chelmsford — all tea and Pimm's. The amount of times Steve Waugh said to me: 'Enjoy it Nasser, this is your last Test. We will never see you again.' *Nasser Hussain warms to Aussie sledging* •982

Man, it don't matter where you come in to bat, the score is still zero.

Madras, 1983. Viv Richards to Sunil Gavaskar after the India captain dropped himself down to No4. He came in with India 0-2. Gavaskar had the last laugh, scoring 236 not out •983

Hell, Gatt, move out of the way, I can't see the stumps. *Dennis Lillee to Mike Gatting* •984

Captain: I want a fielder right under Hussain's nose.
Ian Healy: That could mean anywhere within three miles.
Nasser, to his credit, found this very amusing •985

Who's this then? Father fucking Christmas?
Jeff Thomson as David Steele emerged for his England début, 1975 •986

Mark Waugh: Fuck me, look who it is. Mate, what are you doing out here? There's no way you're good enough to play for England.

Jimmy Ormond: Maybe not, but at least I'm the best player in my family. *Ashes, 2001* •987

We make a good pair, don't we? I can't fucking bat and you can't fucking bowl.
Robin Smith after hitting Merv Hughes for six amidst a furious bout of Merv sledging •988

Go and deflate yourself, you balloon.
Darryl Cullinan to Shane Warne •989

Warne: I've been waiting for two years to have another bowl at you.
Cullinan: Looks like you spent most of it eating.
Reported by Simon Hughes in **Yakking Round The World** •990

You've got more bloody edges than a broken pisspot.
Fred Trueman to Northants batsman, 1956 •991

So how's your wife, and my kids?

Rodney Marsh to Ian Botham •992

What do you think this is a fucking tea party?
No you can't have a fucking glass of water.
You can fucking wait like the rest of us.
Allan Border to Robin Smith during a hot Trent Bridge Test •993

Hey, hey, hey! I'm fucking talking to you. Come here, come
here, come here... Do that again and you're on the next
plane home, son... What was that? You fucking test me
and you'll see. *Allan Border, in on-pitch exchange with his
fast bowler, Craig McDermott, 1993* •994

I've faced bigger, uglier bowlers than you,
mate; now fuck off and bowl the next one.
Allan Border to the young Angus Fraser •995

I don't mind this lot chirping at me, but you're just the fucking bus driver of this team.

Nasser Hussain to a noisy Justin Langer in 1997, when Langer was a mere sub fielder •996

I don't like you, Reeve. I never have liked you. You get right up my nose, and if you come anywhere near me I'll rearrange yours.

David Lloyd •997

Glen McGrath: Why are you so fucking fat?
Eddo Brandes: Because every time I fuck your wife she gives me a biscuit.

The Australian slip fielders were, apparently, helpless with mirth •998

[He] was all bristle and bullshit and I couldn't make out what he was saying, except that every sledge ended in arsewipe.

Michael Atherton on Merv Hughes, in Opening Up •999

Atherton gave as good as he got. His sledging was always more subtle and intelligent than my basic stuff. It would often take me three overs to understand what he meant.

Merv Hughes admits to a grudging respect for a posh Pommie adversary •1000

***Greg Thomas** (after beating the bat):* It's red, round and weighs about five ounces.

***Viv Richards** (after hammering the next ball out of the ground):* You know what it looks like, now go and fetch it.

My all-time favourite •1001

Playing against a team with Ian Chappell as captain turns a cricket match into gang warfare.
Mike Brearley •1002

The last positive thing England did for cricket was invent it.

Ian Chappell •1003

Greg can be a very patient man, much more diplomatic than either his father or his elder brother. However, if you don't want to hear the truth, then don't ask him for a frank opinion. Greg grew up in a household where frank opinions were served up at breakfast more often than cereal and fruit juice.
Ian Chappell on his younger brother and the dynamics in the Chappell household •1004

I have no respect for him as a cricketer or as a man.
Ian Chappell, 1979, on Tong Greig •1006

The other advantage England have got when Phil Tufnell is bowling is that he isn't fielding.

Ian Chappell •1007

If you don't like me there's a few other people [for me] to chat to anyhow.
Ian Chappell •1008

I really get annoyed with this reverse swing term. It's either an outswinger or an inswinger, isn't it? *Ian Chappell. Er... no.* •1009

Chappell was a coward. He needed a crowd around him before he would say anything. He was sour like milk that had been sitting in the sun for a week.

Ian Botham on Ian Chappell •1010

He has been an exciting player to watch in all he did but one cannot discard his long, consistent history of unfortunate behaviour which suggest that his judgement often went astray.
Jack Pollard on Ian Chappell, **Australian Cricket *(1982)*** •1011

There are some things about Ian Chappell I shouldn't have copied, like the way he always used to refuse to sign autographs in a bar. Here was me, 18, telling 50-year-olds to stuff off.

David Hookes, Australian batsman, 1983 •1012

So what is the essence of the game?
Do we know, after all the Cricket Wit
we've just digested? Probably not.
Or maybe it is just about a field, some
players, and twenty-two yards of mown.

The wicket is still being blamed.
It has been libelled, slandered and
blasphemed, accused in turn of
being a fickle and vicious Jezebel
and a slumbering, lifeless old dog.
David Foot, **Cricket's Unholy Trinity** *(1985)* •1013

Official hospitality is an organised conspiracy to prevent the uninterrupted watching of cricket, based upon a constant invitation to 'have a drink' or 'meet our sales manager from Slough.'
Roy Hattersley, The Guardian, *1983* •1014

When you come as a sponsor, you are treated like royalty, I'd recommend it to anyone. When you come as a member on Test-match Saturday, you are shunted around as some species of sub-human. *Douglas Lever, Lancashire member and sponsor* •1015

There should have been a last line of defence during the war. It would have been made up entirely of the more officious breed of cricket stewards. If Hitler had tried to invade these shores he would have been met by a short, stout man in a white coat who would have said, "I don't care who you are, you're not coming in here unless you're a member." *Ray East* •1016

Of all English cricket grounds, Edgbaston is the only one which gives the immediate feeling of being a stadium, an amphitheatre.
George Plumptre, Homes of Cricket *(1988)* •1017

Edgbaston was awash with social inadequates, bawling, brawling, caterwauling; slating, baiting, hating. (It) was a cave of sullen youths, for whom insolence, ugliness and selfishness are basic facts of life.

Michael Henderson, The Times, *1998* •1018

A lotus land for batsman, a place where it was always afternoon and 360 for 2 wickets. *Neville Cardus on Trent Bridge* •1019

I suppose if you don't play in gloom up here, you never play at all.

Alan Knott at Old Trafford, 1981 •1020

More reported cases of frostbite than any other first-class venue.

Jonathan Agnew on playing at Derby in early-season •1021

277

Canterbury in its festival finery is the nearest thing to a pre-war tableau from one of those summers when the sun always shone and the ball scorched just wide of cover point's right hand to the ropes.

David Foot, The Guardian *reprinted in* Waiting for Cheltenham *(1989)* •1022

In some ways Cheltenham is a glorious anachronism and one would be forgiven for wondering how it has survived into the world of late-20th century county cricket.

George Plumptre, Homes of Cricket *(1988)* •1023

Whatever the strict details of geography may insist, Sussex cricket is essentially cricket-by-the-sea. Spiritually this means cricket of holiday atmosphere.

N.W.D. Yardley and J.M. Kilburn, Homes of Sport — Cricket *(1952)* •1024

Certainly there can be few more picturesque grounds, surmounted as it is by the cathedral on the banks of the River Severn to the east, and to the west the distant Malvern Hills.

Rev Hugh Pickles on the County Ground at Worcester, County Champions (1982) •1025

The season of 1896 was to me one of vast interest. It marked my first acquaintance with Plato and Fenners. *G.L. Jessop* •1026

Mote Park, Maidstone… with its 'tall, ancestral trees' [is] captivating; but cricketers have no more appreciation of foliage than the foxhunters of violets in bloom. *J.A.H. Catton in* Bat and Ball *(Ed. Thomas Moult), 1935* •1027

The social side of Kent cricket possesses some of the carnival spirit of the Continent, for each town is gay with bunting, illuminations, and entertainment. Nevertheless St Lawrence has the atmosphere of old times and the countryside. Marquees and tents, decorated and bright with flowers, are near the boundaries, with trees towering behind them. *J.A.H. Catton* •1028

The latest news is that the Hill at Sydney is to be replaced by a stand. So much the better.

E.W. Swanton, 1977 •1029

At The Oval, men seem to have rushed away with some zest from their City offices. At Lord's there is a dilettante look, as of men whose work, if any, has yet to come.

Rev. James Pycroft, Oxford Memories, *1886* •1030

A day sitting in a deckchair in the sun, preferably with at least one similarly inclined companion to while away the longueurs between overs, seems to me a very civilised way of spending one's time. *Tim Heald* •1031

Cricket grounds are like seaside resorts. They come alive in the summer with the sunshine and the deck chairs and the bunting and the bands, but like seaside resorts I find them oddly appealing out of season when they are empty and windswept. *Tim Heald* •1032

My immediate reaction was 'How on earth can major cricket be played on this?'
Jim Fairbrother, Lord's groundsman, on his first sight of the slope, in Testing The Wicket, *1985* •1033

It's still weird when you walk through the Long Room and they're all in jackets and ties. I reckon they should put some jeans on. *Darren Gough on MCC members, 2001* •1034

Whichever side it may be — and I fancy Eton were the principal offenders — the growing tendency to ebullitions of affection and exuberance in the field must be severely checked. They are not pretty at Wembley, but at Lord's quite intolerable. *G.M.H.C. voices his disgust* •1035

The general atmosphere of Lord's is more like a prayer meeting than a ball game. *Alistair Cooke* •1036

Lord's has something no other cricket ground quite possesses. There is an enveloping atmosphere of tradition and peace about the place.

J.H. Fingleton, **The Ashes Crown the Year** *(1954)* •1037

Australians will always fight for those 22 yards. Lord's and its traditions belong to Australia just as much as to England.

John Curtin, Australian prime minister, 1945 •1038

Sir — Now I know that this country is finished. On Saturday, with Australia playing, I asked a London cabby to take me to Lord's and had to show him the way.

Letter to **The Times** •1039

Lord's is the Valhalla of cricketers; countless days, famous for great deeds, have come to a resting place at Lord's.

Sir Neville Cardus, **The Summer Game** *(1929)* •1040

This is, of course, something much more considerable than a place where cricket of the highest calibre is played and watched. It is nothing less than an international institution as well, because of its history and because of what it represents.

Geoffrey Moorhouse, Lord's *(1983)* •1041

BIBLIOGRAPHY

The Art of Captaincy
Brearley, Mike, **Hodder & Stoughton,** *1985*

The Big Book of More Sports Insults
L'Estrange, Jonathan (ed.) **London: Weidenfeld & Nicolson,** *2005*

A Century of Great Cricket Quotes
Hopps, David (ed.), **London: Robson Books,** *2000*

Great Cricket Quotes
Hopps, David (ed.), **London: Robson Books,** *2006*

The Oxford Dictionary of Humorous Quotations
Sherrin, Ned (ed.), **Oxford: Oxford University Press,** *2005*

Sporting Wit: Athletic Wisecracks and Champion Comebacks
Chichester: Summersdale, *2005*

The Times Book of Quotations
Glasgow: Times Books, *2000*

The Wisden Book of Cricket Quotations

Wisden Cricket Annual (various editions)

Various websites were of great help;
online newspaper sites and cricinfo.com especially.